SECRETS

OF

HYPNOTISM

by

Dr. S. J. van Pelt

President of the British Society of Medical
Hypnotists; Editor of the British Journal of Medical
Hypnotism; Member of the British Medical
Association; Member of the National Association
for Mental Health; Member of the Society for
Clinical and Experimental Hypnosis (New York);
Member of the Society for the Study of Addiction
to Alcohol and Other Drugs

Foreword by
MELVIN POWERS

Published by
Melvin Powers
WILSHIRE BOOK COMPANY
12015 Sherman Road
No. Hollywood, California 91605
Telephone: (213) 875-1711

'*Secrets of Hypnotism*'
was first published in 1958 by
Neville Spearman Limited

Copyright 1958
by
WILSHIRE BOOK COMPANY

Printed by

HAL LEIGHTON PRINTING COMPANY
P.O. Box 3952
North Hollywood, California 91605
Telephone: (213) 983-1105

CONTENTS

PART I

WHAT HYPNOTISM IS

PART II

THE BENEFITS OF HYPNOTISM

Chapter		Page

PART III

SOME INTERESTING CASES IN DETAIL

CONTENTS

ILLUSTRATIONS

FOREWORD

Only a student of hypnotic literature can realize how rarely is presented a theory of hypnotism. There are thousands of case studies and interesting analyses of hypnotism, but theories as to the nature of the phenomenon are seldom encountered. Dr. S. J. van Pelt, president of the British Society of Medical Hypnotists, is one of the few persons qualified to present a theory on this subject. He says, "Hypnosis is a concentrating of the various mental activities into a single ray, as it were." The use of mirrors in concentrating terrific beams of solar energy gives you the analogy needed to understand his statement.

Dr. van Pelt believes a genius is simply a person who has the unusual ability to concentrate his mental powers along a single line of endeavor. The average person cannot become a genius because of the many "brain barriers" or habits of negative beliefs already set up in his mind. To put it more simply, the average person does not think of himself as a genius, and therefore, will never try to become one. What is thought to be impossible, actually becomes impossible.

This brings us to Dr. van Pelt's "3-D Technique" in which he states imagination, rather than the will, is what is important in the hypnotic process. It is the mental picture the subject sees, and not his effort of will that is important in a self-improvement program. People are usually discouraged from trying to improve themselves because of the tremendous amount of will-power they feel will be needed. This is a great mistake. If a person changes his mental self-image to what he would like to be, his "will" falls into line and begins to mould him in that direction. Thus, the will-power element in self-improvement is automatically present. Since self-improvement requires motivation, effort, and visualization, hypnotism can help anyone interested in this type of program. But what of the person who tries several times to achieve his goal, believing in himself all the time — and yet fails? Dr. van Pelt encourages that person by stating that the unsuccessful trials made to date are not a fair sample of what his life can ultimately become. In fact, his chances for success are greatly augmented by using techniques of self-hypnosis. Worthwhile goals are usually not achieved overnight.

You will find Dr. van Pelt's comments on the value of hypnosis in space travel most timely. Case histories showing how hypnotism was used with excellent results will keep your interest high to the last page of this extremely interesting book.

Melvin Powers

12015 Sherman Road
No. Hollywood, California 91605

PREFACE

IN RESPONSE TO numerous requests, it has been decided to re-publish in book form material from lectures, numerous articles from the *British Journal of Medical Hypnotism*, and small books by the author which have been out of print for some time, thus making readily available to the reader material which, for the most part, could still be found only in the scientific, medical and leading university libraries of the world.

In the past, ignorance, superstition, sensational stories of the Svengali-Trilby type, misleading but spectacular performances by 'quacks,' and the pompous pronouncements of even some psychiatrists with no real practical knowledge of the subject have all combined to create a wrong impression in the public and professional mind concerning hypnotism.

This has hindered the development of a great scientific truth, which could be of inestimable benefit to mankind. For hypnotism is a science. Whatever else may be said about it, unlike the theories of Freud, which can never be proved, the effects obtainable under hypnosis can be, and have been frequently, demonstrated scientifically.

For instance, millions of people have seen the painless extraction of a tooth under hypnosis on television. Years ago the photographs in this book, depicting a similar operation, were published in the *British Journal of Medical Hypnotism*. That anaesthesia can be produced by hypnotic suggestion is therefore a proved fact. Likewise all the other remarkable effects obtainable under hypnosis can be demonstrated and proved beyond a shadow of a doubt.

The photograph of the electrocardiogram in this book shows that even the heart rate can be influenced by hypnotic suggestion. This particular piece of research by the author was carried out several years before it was published in

Experimental Hypnosis, a symposium of hypnotic research, in 1952.

It is a fundamental requirement of science that theories should be capable of proof. Hypnotism passes that severe test. It is a proved fact that neurosis can be artificially induced by hypnotic suggestion, as evidenced by the experimental work of Luria in Russia. It is equally well established that this deliberately induced neurosis can be removed by hypnotic suggestion. Therefore we have the perfect example of a controlled experiment. Is it not logical to assume that modern hypnotism can help therefore both to explain and treat what may be called 'ordinary,' or naturally occurring, nervous and allied disorders, and so bring health and happiness?

The cases described in this book are very simple, but they illustrate great scientific principles. The author claims originality for the theory that hypnotic suggestion plays a role in causing nervous and allied disorders, the method of treatment by light hypnosis, according to the principles of the three 'Rs'—Relaxation, Realisation, and Re-education—and the theory of the nature and mechanism of the hypnotic state, and the reason for increased suggestibility and response to suggestion in this state.

So far no scientist has been able to refute these theories scientifically, and they explain what has hitherto largely been regarded as inexplicable.

A certain amount of overlap is inevitable in a composite work of this kind. This has been reduced to a minimum by the careful editing of Mr. Gavin Gibbons, and the help given by my publishers, to both of whom the author extends his grateful thanks for making these collected papers readily available to those who want to know the truth about hypnotism, and the modern method of using it.

S. J. VAN PELT, M.B., B.S.

Harley Street,
London, W.1.

Chapter One

HYPNOTISM AND ITS IMPORTANCE IN MEDICINE*

THERE ARE ALMOST as many theories concerning the nature of hypnotism as there are hypnotists. Some, like Charcot, believe hypnosis to be pathological and a mere symptom of hysteria. There is no evidence to support this, unless 80–90 per cent of the people can be regarded as hysterical. Physiological theories attribute it to anything from cerebral anaemia to a special function of the autonomic nervous system. Pavlov believed that hypnosis and sleep were identical. This is a common belief, but all physiological tests prove that hypnosis is more characteristic of the waking state than sleep. The word 'sleep' is commonly used to describe the trance state, but it means hypnotic sleep, not ordinary sleep.

For instance, the following show some of the differences between sleep and hypnosis:

A person asleep does not respond to stimuli the way a hypnotised person will.

Consciousness is suspended in sleep, but present in hypnosis. Reflexes, such as the knee jerk, which are diminished or abolished in sleep are present in hypnosis.

Electrocardiographic and respiratory studies show that the state is more like normal consciousness than sleep.

Brain potentials in trance are characteristic of the waking state.

The psycho-galvanic reflex is the same as in the waking state (unless a sleep-like state has been suggested).

In this test the resistance of the body to a small current is measured, and it changes under the influence of emotion. Normally, it is about 5,000 ohms.

A prick with a pin causes it to fall to 4,000 ohms and then swing back. In ordinary sleep it may rise to 40,000 or 50,000

---

* *Delivered as a lecture to University College, London, 19 May, 1949.*

3

ohms. In hypnosis it is 5,000 ohms, the same as in the waking state (unless a sleep-like state has been especially suggested).

Another well-known theory was that of dissociation—various functions of the brain being split off from one another by suggestions. Janet thought that a dissociated memory or group of memories might develop into a sort of second personality. Psychiatrists like to think that the subject projects his desire for magical power on to the hypnotist. Another school of thought thinks that the subject regards the hypnotist as a stern father or a kind mother.

Most authorities favour the theory that hypnosis is a state of exaggerated suggestibility. Even in the waking state most people are suggestible. A single word or phrase can make a person feel happy, sad, angry or afraid, and often evoke the bodily symptoms which accompany these feelings. Yawning is notoriously infectious. One person faints in a crowd, and others do likewise.

An idea implanted in the mind tends to realise itself unless definitely inhibited. Consider how a person will make motions with the hand in describing a spiral staircase.

In ordinary waking suggestion the patient can use the inhibiting influence, but in hypnosis this is abolished. Once induced, the effects of hypnosis are mechanical, and operate whether the patient believes it or not.

For all practical purposes it is easiest to regard hypnosis as a peculiar psychical state where the mind is particularly susceptible to suggestion.

The Author's Theory

The author believes that hypnosis is really a superconcentration of the mind. In the ordinary state the mind is occupied with many different impressions, so that the mind power is scattered. Therefore any suggestion given in this condition 'goes in one ear and out the other.' Only a small part of the mind absorbs it, and therefore the effect is weak.

In hypnosis the mind is concentrated to a degree much higher than possible in the ordinary state. Practically all the suggestion is absorbed, and so the effect is strong.

In 100 per cent concentration or very deep hypnosis, there will be no mind power left free to take notice of anything except what is suggested, and the subject will be oblivious to severe pain.

After hypnosis, when the mind returns to its usual state, each 'unit of mind power' will carry a dose of suggestion, and the patient will get the appropriate feelings.

You will see how this theory can explain the extraordinary effects which are obtainable under hypnosis, and which up to now have been considered unexplainable. (See Diagram 1.)

However much controversy there may be concerning the exact nature of hypnosis, a great deal more is known about what may be called the practical side of the subject—that is, who can hypnotise, how hypnosis can be induced, who can be hypnotised, and what phenomena may be expected.

Now in the interests of science and truth, something must be said which few hypnotists would admit—at least publicly— because it would destroy their prestige, and, as you will see later, prestige is important. The fact is that the hypnotist possesses 'no mysterious gift' or 'hypnotic power' whatever.

Such a power, if it can be called that, lies within the subject— the hypnotist merely has the technical knowledge of how to manipulate it.

Anybody can learn to hypnotise. Unfortunately, the easiest subjects to hypnotise are those who 'sleep' very deeply. In the hands of amateur hypnotists and stage performers who have no medical knowledge, such people may suffer considerable mental harm.

Only recently a letter was received from a mother concerning her daughter's nervous breakdown. She wrote: 'her complaint followed a stage performance by ——, during which she was hypnotised several times.' Hypnosis demands the utmost care and attention on the part of the operator. In the rush and excitement of a stage performance, the operator may forget to countermand suggestions, and so set up a serious neurosis in susceptible subjects. The proper place for hypnotism is in the consulting room. It is no more suitable for the stage than any other branch of medicine. For this reason, public performances of hypnotism are not favoured, particularly as most performers dabble in medical treatment.

Since the power or ability to be hypnotised lies within the patient, it becomes easier to understand why some people

THE NATURE OF HYPNOSIS

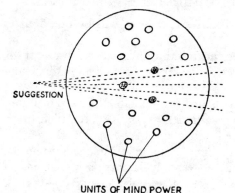

ORDINARY STATE

Only a few 'Units' affected by Suggestion, therefore effect is weak.

SUGGESTION

UNITS OF MIND POWER

Scattered units of mind power untouched by suggestion.

HYPNOSIS

Units of mind power concentrated and all affected by suggestion, therefore strong effect.

No mind power left to take notice of anything apart from the hypnotic suggestion, therefore even pain is ignored.

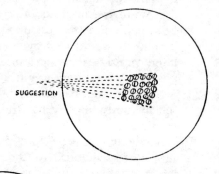

SUGGESTION

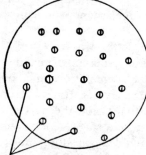

Units of mind power scattered again but now each carries a dose of suggestions.

AFTER HYPNOSIS

UNITS OF MIND POWER WITH A DOSE OF SUGGESTION

Diagram 1

This diagram shows that hypnosis is not sleep or unconsciousness but a superconcentration of the mind. It explains clearly why suggestion is more powerful in hypnosis than in the ordinary state.

(By courtesy of the *British Journal of Medical Hypnotism*)

make better subjects than others, and also why there are degrees of hypnotism.

People vary in their susceptibility to hypnosis the way they do to drugs and other forms of medical treatment generally.

Statistics show that 80–90 per cent of all people can be hypnotised.

Generally accepted figures are as follows:

> Uninfluenced, 5 per cent or less;
> Hypnoidal state, 10 per cent;
> Light trance, 25 per cent;
> Medium trance, 35 per cent;
> Somnambulistic trance, 25 per cent.

This does not necessarily mean the results obtained at the first attempt.

Some people who can be only lightly influenced at first can be trained to become good subjects by repeated sessions.

Hypnosis follows the laws of habit formation, and becomes easier with repeated sessions.

The maximum depth of trance which can be reached will come in eight to twelve sittings, provided they are not too far apart.

The usual belief is that a person must be 'weak-willed' to be hypnotised. Actually, this is quite wrong. The 'will' has nothing to do with hypnotism, except the ordinary willingness to co-operate, and in some cases even this is not necessary.

In hypnotism we deal with the imagination—indeed, it has been described as a 'manipulation of the imagination.'

The imagination is stronger than the will. In any contest between the two the imagination will always win, as the following experiment will show.

Place a plank of wood on the floor and anybody can walk along it. Raise it in the air a few feet, between supports, and few people can do it, because they think, or imagine, that they would get giddy and fall. While they are in this state of mind, all the will-power in the world can't help them, or stop them from falling.

The best hypnotic subjects are ordinary, normal people, the more intelligent and imaginative they are the better. It is practically impossible to hypnotise an idiot. Nervous and neurotic people are often difficult at first. Children usually make good subjects owing to their powers of imagination. Young people between the ages of eighteen and twenty-six are better than older people, as they are not so set in their ways. There is no difference between the sexes in their reaction to hypnosis.

Sceptical people are often easy subjects, because secretly they believe in hypnosis, while openly expressing doubt.

On the other hand, many people who openly express their desire for hypnotism secretly believe that to yield would show they were 'weak-minded'—therefore they resist subconsciously.

Saying 'I can't be hypnotised' is like saying 'I am a dull, stupid person with no imagination and no power of concentration whatsoever.'

Finally, the patient should have a real motive for seeking hypnosis.

A man who really desires to be cured of alcoholism can easily be helped. If he is dragged along by his wife or relatives, and secretly has no desire to stop, then hypnosis is not likely to succeed.

There are certain tests of suggestibility which give a good idea of whether a patient is likely to make a good subject or not.

Suggestibility is not gullibility—the latter implies trickery.

One of the simplest tests is the hand-locking experiment— often described as 'mass hypnotism' by stage hypnotists.

The subjects are told to clasp their hands together and also to imagine strongly that they are locked. In a large audience— especially in a theatre where an emotional atmosphere has been created—there will always be a few people who cannot undo their hands or have great difficulty in doing so when challenged.

Similar tests can be carried out with closure of the eyes and swaying of the body.

People who respond positively to these tests are very likely to make good subjects.

Stage hypnotists take advantage of these tests to pick those people who will make the easiest and best subjects from among volunteers.

As may be expected from the fact that the ability to be hypnotised lies within the patient, there are no hard and fast rules and clear-cut stages.

Every patient is law unto himself, and subjects may show different phenomena at different stages. Some, for instance, may follow post-hypnotic suggestions even after a light trance—others may refuse to do so even after a deep trance. In general, we may describe the following stages as fairly typical:

The Hypnoidal Stage

This consists of mere drowsiness and a heavy sensation in limbs.

The Light Stage

Here we have closure of the eyes, complete relaxation, and inhibition of voluntary movement. The eyelids may quiver a little.

The Medium Trance

This is characterised by automatic obedience, catalepsy of limbs, rigidity, automatic movements, and anaesthesia or analgesia. There may be partial amnesia, and simple post hypnotic suggestions may be carried out.

The Somnambulistic Stage

Here there may be ability to open the eyes without waking—positive and negative hallucinations, complete amnesia and response to bizarre post-hypnotic suggestions.

In the light and medium stages the patient may remember all the events of the trance, and may even doubt that he was really hypnotised, because he could hear the hypnotist speaking.

It is astonishing how many people think that they should be completely 'blacked out' during hypnosis.

Even in the deep trance the subject hears the hypnotist—otherwise he would be unable to follow suggestions.

However, as amnesia often follows the deep trance, the patient imagines he didn't hear anything, as events of the trance have been forgotten.

Another common belief is that the deeper the trance the greater the effect. This is similar to the belief sometimes met with among patients in general medical practice—that if one dose of medicine does good, a double dose will do better!

Those with experience of hypnotic suggestion soon realise that response to suggestion does not necessarily depend upon the depth of trance, and that a great deal of good can be done medically using only the light or medium trance.

Regarding methods of inducing hypnosis here again there are almost as many as there are hypnotists. No one method will suit everybody. Some people want to be dominated, some want to be coaxed, and some 'know it all' types like to think they are doing it all themselves. The hypnotist has to adapt his methods to suit the personality and psychic needs of the patient.

One of the easiest and best-known methods for general purposes is that of eye fixation combined with verbal suggestion. This method does not frighten the patients, and allows them to feel they are co-operating.

Another favourite method, often used by stage performers, is to simply close the eyes and talk 'sleep.' This has the advantage that the really susceptible patients do fall into a trance, and even those unaffected sit with their eyes closed and so impress the audience.

So-called 'quick methods' as used upon the stage often depend upon a trick. Sometimes a ju-jitsu wrestling trick is employed. Pressure is applied over the carotid bodies in the neck and the carotid arteries. A degree of cerebral anaemia results, and consciousness is rapidly lost. As the subject goes limp, the hypnotist shouts 'Sleep' and in many cases this will succeed in throwing the patient into a trance. Even if not in a trance, the subject seldom has any desire for the experiment to be repeated, and is content to give an imitation of a hypnotised person. This method can be dangerous and could easily result in death from vagal inhibition. There was an article in the *Lancet* on 2 April, 1949, on 'Deaths from Vagal Inhibition,' by Dr. Keith Simpson, in which cases were mentioned where death had resulted from pressure on the neck.

Apart from the danger, nervous patients are not likely to relish these violent methods!

In some cases, ordinary sleep can be changed into hypnosis, but obviously the opportunities for this are limited.

Concerning the effects which can be obtained with hypnosis hyper-suggestibility appears to be the most characteristic phenomenon of the trance. The subject seems anxious to please the hypnotist and will carry out suggestions which do not conflict with his basic moral principles.

The subject is not an automaton. He can, and often does, refuse to carry out suggestions. He can always break the trance if the situation becomes really intolerable. The patient has several defences against undesirable suggestions. He may refuse to carry out the order, wake up or go into ordinary sleep.

It is the general consensus of responsible opinion that the hypnotised subject will not commit a really serious crime unless he is of the type who could be persuaded to commit crime in real life.

Subjects do not mind pretending to commit crime—stealing a few pennies or stabbing someone with a paper dagger—because they know very well that it is an experiment, and that the hypnotist is not likely to involve himself in a real crime.

Similarly, an ordinary modest person would refuse to undress completely on the stage, although he may take off his shoes in a spirit of fun.

Of course a strip-tease artiste or an exhibitionist would probably think nothing of it.

Rapport is another phenomenon much talked of in hypnosis.

The subject is supposed to respond solely to the hypnotist. It has been proved that this is not real, but nevertheless, in the majority of cases, the subject does act as if it were.

Muscular changes such as alteration in muscle tone, paralysis, catalepsy and automatic movements can all be brought about.

Any voluntary muscular activity can be increased, decreased or inhibited.

The whole body can even be made rigid and stretched between two chairs, where it will support the weight of the hypnotist.

There is probably no real increase in muscular strength. Experience in electro-convulsant therapy has shown the tremendous strength of the human muscles. Even bones may be broken by the force of the contractions. In ordinary life, the mind imposes a restraint and full muscular strength is not used. The jaw muscles can exert over 600 lb. pressure. Few people ever use this, yet it enables acrobats to hang by their teeth from a trapeze. Hypnotism by removing restraint allows the muscles to act with full strength.

All sorts of sensory changes can be produced—one of the most important being anaesthesia, or, rather, analgesia.

In good subjects this can be very real, and even major operations can be performed.

The special senses such as vision, hearing, taste and smell can all be hallucinated. When told that it is perfume, a patient will be quite undisturbed even by the fumes of strong ammonia.

In deep somnambulism the eyes may be opened and positive and negative visual hallucinations induced.

Tests have been carried out by fastening the eyes open and alternately suggesting blindness and vision. Brain-waves ceased on suggesting the patient could see, and appeared as in a blind person when blindness was suggested.

Automatic writing and crystal gazing are among the interesting phenomena which can be obtained. These have long been regarded by the credulous and superstitious as occult manifestations.

The subject's hand will write quite automatically without the conscious mind being aware of what it is doing.

Some people can do this without being hypnotised by another person. In this case, they may be said to have hypnotised themselves. Although messages are popularly supposed to come from the spirit world, analysis of the rather earthy writings show that they really come from the patient's mind. In the crystal the subject may recall and see scenes which have long been forgotten. These methods are sometimes useful in recovering buried material for the purpose of analysis.

In age regression the subject in trance is taken back to definite periods in early life—even childhood. There is some doubt as to whether this is real or not. Intelligence tests and hand-writing changes seem to support it. Present consensus of opinion is that regression actually does reproduce early behaviour.

Regarding the effect of hypnosis on the time sense there are many reports of experiments in the literature where a patient carried out a post-hypnotic suggestion at exactly the time stated—say 3,240 minutes. Bramwell's experiments have never been duplicated, but it is well known that most people can wake at a definite hour. Everybody passes through a short period of hypnosis just before going to sleep. An order given to the mind in this state is very likely to be carried out. Thus a mother can sleep through the noise of a storm, but will wake at the slightest cry of her baby.

In hypnosis there appears to be an increased control over the autonomic nervous system acting, probably, through the emotions.

Even in the ordinary waking state, emotions can have an effect on the body. For instance, it is common knowledge that if worried a person can get a nervous headache, or nervous palpitation if frightened.

In hypnosis the effects can be controlled and intensified.

It is easy to produce vomiting, for instance.

It has been reported that the blood sugar can be raised by suggesting the intake of sugar. Gastric secretion can be increased by suggesting food. After all, a flow of saliva can be caused by thinking of food in the waking state.

Changes of pulse rate and blood pressure have been reported in response to hypnotic suggestion. Certainly the author has been able to lower blood pressure in his own practice. One medical man has reported a fall in his blood pressure after hypnotic suggestion, and he was a very poor hypnotic subject. There is much room for research in this important field. These changes are brought about through the emotions rather than by direct suggestion.

The post-hypnotic suggestion is one of the most important phenomena in hypnosis. After waking the patient carries out a suggestion which has been given during the trance. The suggestion will be carried out with remarkable accuracy. If the trance has been deep enough and the amnesia is complete, then the patient will carry out the suggestion without even knowing why he is doing it. Having performed the act, the patient will often rationalise to explain his seemingly absurd action. For instance if told to take a shoe off, he may do so. If asked why, he will probably say 'Oh, it was a bit tight,' or 'My foot ached, and I wanted to give it a rest.'

Often the suggestion can be resisted, but only at considerable trouble, and the patient feels vaguely unhappy until he has carried out the suggestion.

Use is made of the post-hypnotic suggestion in treatment, and also to make succeeding hypnotic sessions easier. A patient can be trained to fall into a hypnotic sleep at any prearranged signal, thus giving not only quick but instantaneous hypnosis.

Stage hypnotists often make use of this knowledge, and have one or two well-trained subjects who mingle with the volunteers. These people can be hypnotised quickly and easily, and so impress the others.

Amnesia is characteristic of the deep somnambulistic trance, although it may not always be complete. There may be partial amnesia after even a medium trance. Experiments with conditioned reflexes would seem to show that it is not real. Nevertheless after a deep trance patients usually have no memory for events during hypnosis. This is especially so if amnesia is suggested by the hypnotist. In the trance events during the previous session, for which there was no memory on waking, can be recalled and the amnesia can be broken down by persistent questioning and association of ideas even in the waking state. It was Freud's observation of Bernheim's experiments in this direction which led to psychoanalysis.

Let us now consider how hypnotism may be used for medical purposes.

Hypnotism and Direct Symptom Removal

Here the patient is hypnotised and told that his particular complaint will trouble him no more. Psychiatrists criticise this method, saying that as the cause has not been discovered the patient will relapse.

Hypnoanalysis

Here hypnotism is used to shorten the process of psycho-analysis. If use is to be made of amnesia, age regression and recall of repressed memories, a deep trance is necessary. This limits the method to those patients who can be hypnotised deeply.

Hypnotism with Direct and Indirect Suggestion and Re-education of the Patient.

The value of this method is that it will succeed with only light to medium hypnosis, which 80–90 per cent of people can achieve. Further, it gives the patient some insight into his problems, and enables him to adjust himself to life. As there is no amnesia, the patient understands perfectly well why he is doing certain things. This allows him to feel that he is co-operating and increases his self-confidence. Few patients relish the idea of acting like automatons. In this method, hypnotism is used as a sort of mind training.

Hypnosis may be regarded as the key to the mind of man. Neuroses, illusions, delusions and hallucinations can all be induced experimentally under hypnosis and as quickly removed.

Surely such a powerful weapon must be of the utmost importance in investigating the cause of mental disorders. Yet at a recent International Congress on Mental Health, attended by two thousand delegates from more than fifty countries, no mention was made of hypnotism.

Personally, the author is inclined to believe that most nervous disorders are due to a form of self-hypnosis. Consider, for instance, a case of hysterical blindness. A soldier may be cut over the eyes by a shell splinter. The blood runs into his eyes so that he can't see. His mind is in a highly emotional state—and we know that emotion sensitises the mind to hypnosis. The explosion has driven all thoughts out of his head except the one dominant thought which flashes through his mind, 'My eyes, I can't see, I'm blind.' In many cases he will be blind. In other words, he has induced blindness by self-hypnosis, just as a hypnotist could induce blindness in a susceptible person. He will remain blind until de-hypnotised by some process, either a shock of sufficient magnitude or a hypnotist. In some cases, if he has sufficient faith, Christian Science, faith healing, spirit healing or a 'miracle' at some famous shrine may work a cure.

All of these methods use hypnotism in a crude, unscientific way without even knowing it—indeed they often loudly proclaim it to be the work of the Devil!

Nevertheless, it cannot be denied that there are occasional cases of 'cures' after orthodox methods have failed.

Psychiatrists are hard put to it to explain these cures in the light of their theories, but hypnotism explains them easily.

After all, excluding organic disease, there is little difference between the person in an asylum who thinks he is Napoleon and a hypnotised person on the stage who believes he is the same gentleman. The stage Napoleon can be quickly restored to normal, because he is under the control of the hypnotist. Napoleon in the asylum has hypnotised himself, and is therefore difficult to de-hypnotise. Nevertheless, Lindner, in *Rebel Without Cause*, describes the successful treatment of a criminal psychopath by hypnosis.

Whether you believe this theory or not, the practical fact is that hypnosis is extremely useful in the treatment of the following types of cases: *psycho-neuroses, neurasthenia, anxiety state, hysteria, obsessional neurosis* and *depression.*

Secondly, it may be useful to remove the nervous element which is present in many cases of organic disease. By removing fear and worry and inducing relaxation, hypnosis can help in conditions known as 'stress diseases'—angina pectoris, high blood pressure, asthma, duodenal ulcer, etc. Doctors often tell the patient to 'relax,' but they don't tell him how. Hypnotism can teach the patient to relax utterly and completely mind and body.

Hypnosis can often make the mind easier and relieve pain in incurable disease and prolonged and painful illnesses.

Bad habits, such as alcoholism, excessive smoking, sexual perversions, bed-wetting, will all respond well to hypnotism. Painful and obscure conditions such as migraine, trigeminal neuralgia, phantom limb and cardiospasm can often be relieved.

Skin disease, where there is a big nervous element, will respond to hypnotism. Such conditions as neurodermatitis, rosacea, eczema, urticaria and psoriasis are suitable for this method, also any obviously neurotic skin complaints such as dermatitis artefacta and pruritus. Even warts have responded to suggestion.

There is a limited use for hypnotism as an anaesthetic in selected cases. It can be used to ensure painless child-birth in suitable cases. The patient should be trained by several sessions beforehand, if possible. In some cases it may be used as an anaesthetic in dentistry. Even when anaesthesia cannot be obtained it may be useful to reassure nervous patients.

Typical clinical cases which have responded to hypnotism.

Anxiety State

The patient, a young man, was sent for treatment by his doctor. He had been invalided out of the Service and was alleged to suffer from epilepsy. Following an outburst which got him into trouble with the authorities, he was sent to hospital for examination. There he was diagnosed as a severe case of anxiety neurosis.

When seen, the patient seemed very nervous and 'down at heel' in appearance. He stated that he thought his trouble started when war broke out. On being called up, he had endeavoured to hide his extreme fear. This, he thought, he had managed to do, until someone said: 'What are you shaking for?' From then on, he thought everybody could see he was a coward, and as a result he avoided everybody. Even when invalided, he felt ashamed of himself, said he could not face anybody, and was unable to work, and he shook so much. The patient was hypnotised six times, at weekly intervals, with complete success. Even at the fourth treatment, the patient appeared, neatly dressed, and confidently announced that he was back at work.

Claustrophobia—Married woman, 70

This patient was sent along by her doctor because she suffered severely from claustrophobia, which caused her to experience great distress in any situation where she felt she could not easily escape. Thus, travelling by train was impossible for her. She had already had six months' orthodox psychiatric treatment with no result, and the doctor considered that, in view of her age, a quicker method was more desirable. She was a very poor hypnotic subject, yet after six treatments she was able to return home by train and reported a perfectly calm and pleasant trip. Over a year later she wrote to say that she was still completely free from her old nervous trouble, in spite of the fact that she had had a severe and very trying organic illness.

Anxiety Hysteria

This young man was sent along by his doctor. He had suffered from writer's cramp for a number of years, and had been invalided from the Service. On endeavouring to write, his hand would go into such spasms that he could not write a word. The condition appeared after he had written a rude letter about a superior officer. After several sessions of hypnosis, he was able to write freely, and expressed his intention of writing a book.

Asthma—Young married woman, 30

This patient had suffered from asthma attacks with nasal catarrh and sneezing for a number of years. It soon became apparent that her attacks were due to emotion, as she was jealous of her husband. Some time after hypnotic treatment, she wrote to report that she had been completely free of asthma attacks and catarrh.

Insomnia

The patient was a fully qualified doctor, who specialised in psychiatry. As the result of an operation, his sleep rhythm had been disturbed, and the patient was unable to get refreshing sleep even with large doses of drugs. Being a psychiatrist, he had full insight into his mental condition, but still could not sleep. Only a light hypnosis could be achieved, yet nevertheless after a few sessions the patient was able to sleep the whole night through without drugs.

Emotional Catarrh

The patient, a young married man, had suffered from this for a number of years. The condition arose after an emotional upset with his wife, but it was completely cleared up by hypnosis in six weekly sessions.

Nail Biting—Young man of 21

The patient was highly nervous, and had been badly treated when young by people whom he would have dearly loved to strike back. This being impossible, he had bottled up his aggression, which he expressed by biting his nails. After several sessions of hypnosis he was able to give up this habit and took pride in the care of his nails.

Excessive Smoking

The patient was a well-educated professional woman who smoked excessively. After several treatments she stated that she had given up cigarettes without any hardship. Some time later she wrote to state that the cure had been maintained.

Another patient was a fully qualified medical specialist, who wished to give up smoking, as he realised that it was detrimental to his health. After several sessions he reported that he had been able to give up cigarettes without any hardship.

Obscure Skin Complaint

This patient was a young married woman who had suffered from a mysterious skin complaint for a number of years. She attributed it to worry and anxiety during the war. She had seen several skin specialists, and even had sections of skin removed for examination in a leading hospital without beneficial results. Everybody proclaimed it to be a mystery and advised her to forget about it! Some time after a course of hypnosis she wrote to say that the rash had entirely gone.

Rheumatism (nervous or hysterical origin)

The patient was a married woman who developed intense pains in the back and down the legs. As later events showed, this was due to a nervous upset, as the result of trouble with her husband. The nervous origin not being recognised, the patient had been subjected to the most severe treatment, including an operation on the spine. When first seen, she was wearing a spinal support and could barely walk without the aid of two sticks. After several sessions of hypnosis, she was able to discard the spinal support and walk up several flights of stairs unaided.

Another patient was a young girl who complained of severe aches and pains all over her body, particularly the back of the neck, shoulder and arm. One leg was also affected. She wanted to get married, but said that she felt so miserable that she could not do so in her present condition. It was soon revealed that her condition was due to muscular spasms, as the result of the nervous tension generated by pent-up emotion, worry and anxiety. A few sessions of hypnosis were sufficient to remove this tension, and, as a result, she lost all the pains and aches.

Stammering

The patient was a professional man who had stammered all his life. He was a difficult hypnotic subject, and explained that a famous stage hypnotist, now dead, had tried to hypnotise him without success. It was explained that deep hypnosis was not necessary for medical purposes, and after several sessions of light hypnosis he wrote to say he was completely cured.

Blushing

The patient was a young man who blushed on the slightest provocation. He could not face anybody without going scarlet. Naturally, he felt terribly embarrassed, and could not take part in any social functions. He explained that his misery was out of all proportion to his complaint. Several sessions of light hypnosis enabled him to gain complete control, so that he no longer blushed or felt embarrassed.

Sex Habits

The patient was a young man who was addicted to masturbation. In spite of advice from a psychologist 'not to worry,' he stated that he could not help feeling ashamed, especially as he wanted to get married. Half a dozen sessions of hypnosis were sufficient to cure him of this habit and restore his self-respect.

Migraine

The patient was a married woman who had suffered from migraine attacks regularly every two weeks for thirty years. They had begun at the age of ten, and continued in spite of all medical and surgical treatment. Hypnosis soon broke this sequence, and the patient went for two months and then had a very mild attack. Treatment was continued, and in six months the patient had only three slight attacks. At the time of writing, she has been free for some considerable time, and now appears to be cured.

. . . . .

Hypnotism is definitely not a 'cure all,' but there are few cases which cannot benefit from its use.

Once prejudice has been overcome, there is no reason why hypnotism should not be used in appropriate cases together with other medical treatment.

For instance, a patient with high blood pressure is told

to relax. This he often finds it very difficult or impossible to do. Hypnotism will enable him to do this, with consequent benefit to his condition.

People who ridicule the idea that mere words can affect bodily functions should remember that even waking suggestions can cause changes in organs and glands in any part of the body which can be affected by emotion.

Words can have definite physical effects working through the emotions.

If suggestion can cause blood to rush to the face, as in blushing, there is no logical reason why it should not be able to increase the blood supply to the legs, as in a case of thromboangiitis obliterans.

There is a vast field for research in hypnosis and its application to medicine. When we consider that a wart, which is only a growth, can be made to disappear by suggestion, it opens up the fascinating possibility that we may be able to influence other growths. It is merely a bare possibility, and only years of painstaking work, experiment and research can supply the answer. There can be no harm in trying it in cases which have been given up as hopeless.

Let us end this chapter by quoting John Elliotson, who was one of the most brilliant men of his time in English medicine. He was Professor of Medicine, and one of the founders of University College Hospital, London. Although he introduced the stethoscope to England, together with the methods of examining the heart and lungs, which are used to this day, he was forced to resign his position because he experimented with mesmerism. Answering the Dean of the University at that time, who urged him to give up mesmerism, Elliotson replied in the words which should be our guiding principle today:

'The Institution was established for the discovery and dissemination of Truth. All other considerations are secondary. We should lead the public, not the public us. The sole question is whether the matter is the truth or not.'

Chapter Two

WILL HYPNOTISM REVOLUTIONISE MEDICINE?

LEST THE READER should form the wrong conclusion from the title of this chapter let the writer hasten to explain that he would be the very first to deny that hypnotism is a panacea for all human ills. Nevertheless, it is hoped to show that there is a far greater scope for its use in medicine than is generally recognised.

Nobody, no matter how fanatically he may be opposed to hypnotism, can deny that in this science we have the most powerful and effective method of controlling the mind and, through the mind, the whole body. When a few words, by suggesting paralysis, for instance, can render a hypnotised person powerless to move, although fully conscious and able to reason, who can doubt the power of hypnotism? When hypnotic suggestion can cause the mouth to water, change the heart rate or cause the sweat glands to function, who can fail to be impressed with its possibilities in medicine?

More and more is heard these days of the influence of the mind in medicine, and in an article in the *British Medical Journal* entitled 'In Praise of Idleness,'* the importance of the role it plays in the so-called 'stress diseases'—thyrotoxicosis, duodenal ulcer and non-renal hypertension—was pointed out. Again, in another article, 'The Mind and the Skin,'† in a different issue of the same journal, a long list of skin diseases was given in which the psychogenic factor was stated to play a part. This list included such conditions as acarophobia, dermatitis factitia, trichotillomania, neurodermatitis, pruritus ani and vulvae, atopic eczema, rosacea urticaria, hyperidrosis, cheiropompholyx, seborrhoeic dermatitis, psoriasis and alopecia areata! Nevertheless, in these articles, although the importance of

* *British Medical Journal,* 16 April, 1949. 'In Praise of Idleness,' Sir Heneage Ogilvie, K.B.E., M.Ch., F.R.C.S.

† *British Medical Journal,* 19 March, 1949. 'The Mind and the Skin,' I. B. Sneddon, M.B., M.R.C.P.

the mental factor was clearly shown, no mention was made of the most effective method of controlling the mind. Treatments advocated and discussed varied from major operations to divorce, and giving up work, but the simplest of all treatments, that of medical hypnosis, was not even considered. What is the reason for this attitude? Mainly, of course, it is due to the fact that hypnotism has been given a bad name as the result of crude but spectacular stage performances. One can hardly blame a doctor for hesitating to recommend hypnotism to a patient, for the latter would, more often than not, recoil in horror at the suggestion. Stage performances, often in very bad taste, blatant and wildly extravagant claims of medically ignorant amateur hypnotists, sensational stories of the Svengali-Trilby* type, lurid articles in the Press, foolish radio plays with 'master criminal hypnotists,' and the 'occult' flavour imparted by those who imagine themselves to be 'psychic,' have all combined to present hypnosis as something to be feared and shunned as 'not quite nice' by the majority of people, lay or professional.

Almost as bad is the credulous belief of those who are impressed by the antics of a few stage 'stooges' and who fondly imagine that it is only necessary for the hypnotist to exert his 'amazing power' to 'force' the patient to give up his symptoms. Such people regard hypnotism as some sort of 'magic' and consider that it is sufficient to say 'hocus pocus, now you're well,' in order to cure anything from ingrowing toe-nails to decayed teeth.

Before it can be hoped to make progress with the use of hypnosis in medicine, these foolish ideas must be corrected and hypnosis stripped of all its nonsensical and mysterious trappings, so that it can be presented as a simple, serious and straightforward method of medical treatment. As a first step towards this, some indication of how it 'works' must be given. At lectures to B.M.A. groups, for instance, the writer has often been asked 'How is it that one method of treatment can help cases so widely different?' Doctors are naturally, and quite

* Svengali was a fictional evil character in George Du Maurier's novel *Trilby*. Trilby was an artist's model with a 'voice like a frog' but Svengali hypnotised her to sing like an opera star and had her in his evil power. When Svengali was killed, Trilby dramatically lost her voice—right in the middle of a performance!

rightly, suspicious of anything which claims to be a 'universal cure.' The field in which hypnosis can be useful is so wide that, at first sight, it may appear like claiming that some new 'wonder drug' will cure everything.

However, when the matter is examined more closely, it will be seen that there are sound scientific reasons for using hypnosis in such widely varying conditions. Nobody would deny the importance of the autonomic nervous system and the part it plays in regulating the functions of the body. No organ or gland can work without the appropriate orders from this system. Similarly, nobody can deny that in hypnosis there is a greatly increased control over the autonomic nervous system. This is not just a matter of theory, for such control has been scientifically demonstrated. Even in the waking state it is possible to influence the autonomic system by suggestion. It is well known that it is possible to bring 'tears to the eyes' or 'make the mouth water.' Suitable suggestions can make a person blush or feel angry, sad, happy or afraid and often evoke all the bodily symptoms which accompany these conditions. Of all the phenomena which can be evoked in hypnosis, the one which is common to all stages, even the lightest, is increased suggestibility. Thus we can see that, in hypnosis, even the lightest, we have an increased control over the autonomic nervous system and, indirectly, of all the organs and glands it supplies.

This complex system supplies all those muscles and glands which are not under voluntary control and normally it achieves the desired results without any conscious effort on our part at all.

Such vital processes as the heart action, activity of the sweat glands or digestive processes and dilatation or contraction of the bronchioles and blood-vessels are all under its influence. This whole system, with everything it controls, is profoundly influenced by emotion, so that it is easy to see how vital functions of the body can be affected by hypnotic suggestion. As Fulton* says, 'the heart and circulation may be worked just as hard and just as much as a detriment to the body as a whole from an arm-chair . . . as from a rower's seat.' (See Diagram 2.)

* Fulton, J. F. *Cerebral regulation of Autonomic Function*, Proc. Inter-State Postgrad. Med. Assemb. N.A. 1936A.

HOW IDEAS CAN AFFECT ORGANS AND GLANDS

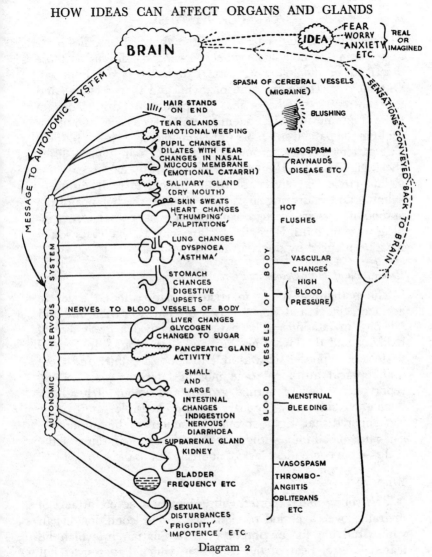

Diagram 2

Purely diagrammatic sketch to show how ideas can affect body organs and cause changes via the autonomic nervous system.

(By courtesy of the *British Journal of Medical Hypnotism*)

With a proper understanding of the above, it becomes more understandable how such widely varying conditions as those described in the following cases can benefit from hypnosis. One factor is common to all of them, and that is FEAR—and fear, no matter of what it may be, produces a disturbance of the autonomic nervous system. Resultant physical symptoms frighten the patient still more until a vicious circle is established. The patient literally becomes 'afraid of the symptoms of fear.' (See Diagram 3.) Hypnosis, properly used, can break this vicious circle and, by enabling the patient to really listen to calming and reassuring suggestion, restores the balance of the autonomic system with a consequent disappearance of unpleasant symptoms. Here, briefly, are some typical cases which have been cured by the right use of hypnosis.

Restoration of Hair Colour and Growth

The patient, a young married woman, suffered a severe accident. Shock and worry caused the hair to turn white and fall out 'in handfuls.' The patient developed a great fear of baldness and the loss of her husband's affection. After several sessions of hypnosis, she was able to adopt a calmer and more philosophical attitude. Some months later she was able to report restoration of normal growth and colour of her hair. Such a result may appear incomprehensible until it is remembered that fright, through its action on the autonomic, can cause blood to be withdrawn from the skin—in this case the scalp—with consequent lack of nourishment to the hair.

Migraine

This young man reported with a history of severe attacks of migraine over a period of eight years. The condition began while studying for an important examination in which he feared failure. Fear of the condition, which had resisted all orthodox methods, including injections, had kept it going. Several sessions of hypnosis with reassurance and relaxation were sufficient to bring about a cure.

Insomnia

The patient, a middle-aged man, reported that he had been unable to sleep without heavy doses of drugs for years. The

HOW A NEUROSIS DEVELOPS

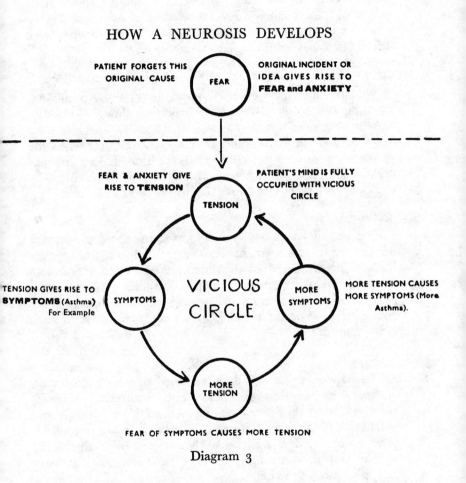

Diagram 3

(By courtesy of the *British Journal of Medical Hypnotism*)

condition followed a period of worry and anxiety over business and domestic affairs. Fear that insomnia would lead to 'madness' had kept it going. Several sessions of hypnosis, during which he was reassured and shown how to relax properly, were sufficient to enable him to sleep without drugs.

Anxiety State

A middle-aged married man complained of severe trembling, sweating and palpitations and a feeling 'as though his inside was turning over' at the slightest excitement. The condition followed a shock at the sudden death of a relative, when the patient developed a great fear of death himself. Explanations and reassurance during several sessions of hypnosis were sufficient to enable him to regain his normal confidence.

Asthma

This patient, a young man, reported that he had suffered from asthma every night for years. Following a heavy, indigestible meal, he had awakened one night and felt 'unable to get his breath.' Fear of this unpleasant feeling had done the rest. After several sessions of hypnosis, he was able to relax completely and sleep naturally, with consequent disappearance of his asthma.

Blushing

The patient, a business man, reported that he had blushed ever since he had been made a fool of by a superior during his early days at work. Fear of looking foolish had so disturbed the balance of his nervous system that he blushed at the slightest provocation. A few sessions of hypnosis were sufficient to enable him to control his feelings easily, with consequent disappearance of the habit.

Enuresis

The patient, a young man, reported that he had wet the bed every night since childhood. He was bitterly ashamed of the condition and was literally afraid to go to sleep. After a few sessions, during which it was explained that fear had kept the condition going, his confidence was restored and he reported some time later that he now slept perfectly dry.

Intermenstrual Haemorrhage

The patient, a young married woman, reported that she had suffered excessive bleeding between the periods for several years. The condition, which had followed a domestic upset, had resisted all medical treatment, and although nothing organic could be discovered the operation of hysterectomy had been advised. After a few treatments she lost her fear of the condition and the periods became normal. An accident some time later caused some irregularity, but this was corrected with a few more sessions of hypnosis. It is common knowledge that suggestion can influence the menstrual cycle. Why not use it scientifically in appropriate cases?

Even in cases of bad habits such as alcoholism or excessive smoking hypnosis can help. Such conditions are usually a result on the part of the patient trying to ease nervous tension and seek relief from its unpleasant effects on the autonomic nervous system. Consider the following typical cases.

Alcoholism

The patient, a married man, complained that he had got into the habit of taking excessive alcohol because he felt 'all strung up' owing to excess of work. Fear of alcoholism only made him worse. When the patient was shown how to relax properly and reassured under hypnosis, he reported himself free of the habit after a few sessions.

Excessive Smoking

The patient, an elderly man, suffered from severe bronchitis and had been advised to give up his heavy smoking. He was unable to do this and feared the ill effects on his health. A few sessions of hypnosis, by removing his fear and enabling him to relax, were sufficient to free him from the habit.

When it is remembered that conditions such as these, and a host of others which are closely allied to them, all respond very simply to hypnotic suggestion, it becomes obvious that there is a very real place in medicine for this valuable method of treatment.

Once prejudice has been overcome and the tremendous scope of hypnotism is realised, then we may expect to see a veritable 'revolution' in medicine. Then, no doubt, patients with insomnia will no longer be merely doped with sleeping tablets but referred to a properly qualified hypnotist for the appropriate treatment.

Those who doubt that mere words can ever take the place of drugs should consider the facts put forward in an article 'Drug Action and Suggestion' in the *British Medical Journal*.* Here it was stated that 'clinically the action of the drug can be profoundly modified by numerous factors arising from the vagaries of the intact patient,' and further that 'the human body reacts not only to physical and chemical stimulation but also to the symbolic stimuli of words and events which have acquired a special significance for the individual.'

* *British Medical Journal*, 7 October, 1950. 'Drug Action and Suggestion.'

Chapter Three

SOME MISCONCEPTIONS ABOUT HYPNOTISM

THIS CHAPTER IS an attempt to clear up some of the misconceptions and fears which surround the subject of hypnotism.
Experience over many years of treating patients reveals that
few indeed come to the consulting room with a clear idea of
what hypnosis really is. It is easy to see from whence their
misunderstanding arises when the usual sources of readily
available information—Press, radio, stage or amateur performances and books of the Svengali-Trilby type—are
considered.

It is well known that if a dog bites a man it is not generally
considered to be of much news value, whereas the reverse
situation is worth headlines that can be read many yards away.
As a result, with very few exceptions, the Press treats the
subject of hypnotism with a sensationalism which does it a
great disservice. Thus we find reports of a person wandering
around in a hypnotic trance for days or climbing up a building
without apparently knowing what he was doing. Such stories
are scarcely likely to inspire confidence in hypnotism as a
medical procedure in the minds of either patients or doctors.
Those who provide material for these stories are usually stage
performers or amateur hypnotists who are more concerned
with personal publicity or self-glorification than furthering
the cause of hypnotism. Almost without exception they claim
that their exhibitions are of great medical value and sadly
explain to sympathetic audiences and naïve reporters how they
regret having to go on making money year after year on the
stage when all they really want is to help suffering humanity
with their precious 'gift.'

They then proceed to hypnotise a few highly suggestible
young people whom they have carefully selected from among
volunteers in the audience by simple tests of suggestibility.

As approximately one person in four is capable of going into a deep trance very quickly and easily, it is not surprising that a few suitable subjects can be obtained from any large audience. Usually the edifying spectacle is then provided of these young people acting as though drunk, or going through various foolish procedures. After this the announcement is made that just as the hypnotist has power to make people do what he suggests, so he has the power over their minds and bodies and can cure illness, both mental and physical, literally at a snap of his fingers.

Such performances and the sensational reports which nearly always follow them are responsible for serious misconceptions in the public mind. Some regard hypnotism as 'a stunt' and place it in the category of stage magic such as the well-known trick of 'sawing a woman in half.' Others, more credulous, consider it the panacea for all human ills, both mental and physical. Such people consider one visit to a hypnotist should be sufficient to clear up complaints of many years' standing which have resisted all other treatments. Occasionally, it is true, there are cases which respond to a single treatment, but by far the majority of long-standing complaints, especially nervous, need far more. This leads naturally to the first question patients usually ask on seeking hypnotic treatment.

The answer to how long the treatment will take depends upon many things, such as the nature of the complaint, response to suggestion, and the method of using hypnosis. Direct suggestion may be used to obtain anaesthesia say for a dental extraction, a deep trance being necessary. (See Illustrations 1, 2 and 4.) If hypnoanalysis, which combines psychoanalysis and hypnosis, is used to treat psychoneurosis, then a hundred hours or more may be necessary. This method, like direct suggestion, demands a deep trance, especially if it is desired to use amnesia, and age regression. Comparatively few people can enter a *deep* trance, and this fact alone constitutes a definite disadvantage to the use of this method. The writer's own particular method aims at an average of four or six treatments. These are usually given at weekly intervals. As only light hypnosis, which fully 90–95 per cent of all people can achieve, is necessary, this method is obviously of considerable practical value as a psychotherapeutic measure. Hypnotism is

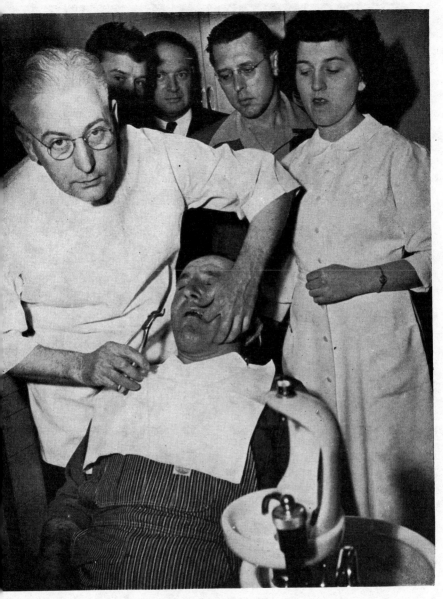

Illustration I (Before)

TOOTH EXTRACTION UNDER HYPNOSIS IN U.S.A.

Picture taken a moment before extraction. Relatively few patients can achieve a sufficient depth of hypnosis for this.

(Photograph by courtesy of the *British Journal of Medical Hypnotism*)

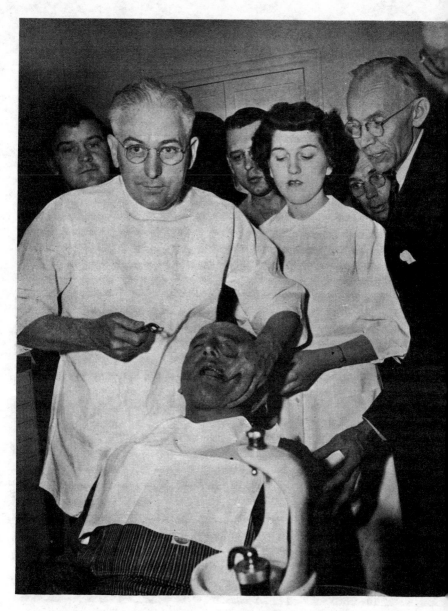

Illustration 2 (After)

TOOTH EXTRACTION UNDER HYPNOSIS IN U.S.A.

Picture taken a moment after extraction.

(Photograph by courtesy of the *British Journal of Medical Hypnotism*)

used as a sort of mind training and the patient is shown how to develop self-confidence and a new method of thinking. In this way he is able to deal not only with his *immediate* problem, but is trained to deal with anything which may crop up in the future. At all times the patient is encouraged to co-operate, and the relationship is that of teacher and student, not master and slave! The patient understands perfectly well from explanations both in and out of trance just what is happening. Few patients really relish acting like automatons and soon come to appreciate a method where two people are working in partnership rather than one dominating the other. The author's original method employs the three 'R's'— *relaxation, realisation* and *re-education*. It works on the principle that what can be caused by suggestion can be cured by suggestion, and really reverses the process which caused all the trouble. First of all a careful history is taken and to one accustomed to this technique the cause of the trouble is often quite obvious even after the first consultation.

Then the patient is taught to relax under light hypnosis. If there has been any difficulty in finding the cause of his trouble he can often remember what first frightened him if instructed to do so under hypnosis. It is quite sufficient to suggest that the thought of what first upset him will come into his head, without trying, some time in the near future.

When the patient realises the cause of his trouble, it can be pointed out that things are different now, so that he no longer needs his old feelings, and can give up being afraid. Then he can be re-educated in order to learn how to face up to his problems in an adult fashion. There are many involved points in technique which cannot be dealt with in detail here, and those who wish to know more are referred to the author's longer works.* When the cause is treated in this way the patient's mind is strengthened and he is no more likely to relapse than an adult is likely to revert to the babyish habit of crawling having once learned to walk. That this method works well in practice is illustrated by the following typical case.

Mr. ——, a middle-aged single man, had suffered from excessive shyness and lack of confidence for many years. As a

---

* *Hypnotism and the Power Within*, Skeffington, London, 10th large ed., 1957. *How to Conquer Nerves*, Skeffington, London, 2nd ed., 1957.

boy he had been rather 'sat upon' and made to feel inferior by the rest of the family. As a result he always felt ill at ease in the company of others, and, as time went on, he began to experience more and more feelings of anxiety. These finally developed into severe 'panic attacks' whenever he was in company. The patient would imagine everybody was looking at him, trembled violently and broke out into a profuse perspiration. As a result of this he avoided social contacts as much as possible and always felt awkward and ill at ease in the presence of others. He kept more and more to himself and felt lonely and depressed. Not understanding the reasons for his feelings, he had a secret fear that there must be something wrong with his mind. The patient proved to be a difficult hypnotic subject, but was able to achieve a light trance at the second attempt. It was pointed out that there was nothing really wrong with his mind, that he had just got into a bad habit of thinking, and that the feelings he got were the usual ones accompanying fear and anxiety.

It was explained to him how his condition had developed into its present state, how he could overcome it, and the idea of complete cure firmly implanted in his mind. At each weekly session the patient reported increased confidence, and after the sixth was able to report that he had been able to take part in several social functions without fear or distress of any kind.

Such a case illustrates the essentially practical nature of light hypnosis and suggestion. The patient was a poor hypnotic subject, and it is unlikely that he could ever have achieved a really deep trance. Certainly he would have been rejected by any stage hypnotist. After his failure to achieve hypnosis at the first attempt the patient was very dejected—nevertheless by persevering he was able to rid himself of a habit which had been ruining his life for many years. All the usual nervous complaints, the so-called psychoneuroses—neurasthenia, anxiety state, hysteria, obsessional neurosis and depression—will respond to hypnosis.

Another remark which patients sometimes make is: 'I doubt if hypnosis can help me, because I am a poor subject.' Inquiry usually reveals the fact that hypnosis has been attempted by some amateur, perhaps a friend, or the patients have volunteered as stage subjects. Not unnaturally, for those

suffering from nervous complaints are seldom the best subjects, they have failed to achieve a deep trance or indeed any
trance at all. As a result they jump to the conclusion that they
cannot be hypnotised, and apply for treatment in a despairing
frame of mind which is not helpful to the hypnotherapist.
Such people fail to realise, until it is pointed out to them, that
there are degrees of hypnosis, and, while it is true that only a
relatively small percentage of people can enter a *deep* trance,
especially at the first attempt, fully 90-95 per cent of all people
can enter a light trance. This is quite sufficient to achieve
excellent results medically, provided the right method is used.
Most people have the idea that a deep trance must be 'more
powerful' than a light trance. Certainly if the more bizarre
phenomena such as positive or negative hallucinations of the
senses are required, then a deep trance will be necessary. All
experienced workers are agreed, however, that response to
therapeutic suggestion does not necessarily depend upon depth
of trance. Some subjects may refuse to carry out suggestions
even after a deep trance, whereas others may respond very
well after a light trance. Increased suggestibility is characteristic
of even the lightest stage of hypnosis, and it is the suggestions
which cure, not the hypnosis. This is illustrated in the following
case.

Mr. ——, aged 60, was a confirmed alcoholic. Recently,
medical reasons had made it desirable for him to give it up.
The patient was rather a 'hard case' and explained that he
did not think hypnotism could do much good as nobody had
been able to hypnotise him. He had gone on the stage as a
volunteer and, of course, had failed to pass the usual tests of
suggestibility. One of his friends had tried many times to
hypnotise him without success. He appeared to approach the
treatment in a spirit of levity, and more as a result of a bet
with his friends than a desire to be cured.

It was explained to him that he could not hope to perform
tricks such as he had seen certain carefully selected subjects
carry out on the stage, but that he could be hypnotised, if he
wished, to a degree sufficient for medical purposes. He
expressed his disbelief but agreed to co-operate. Naturally, he
proved to be a very difficult case and only a light hypnosis
state could be obtained at the first session. At the end of the

session the patient expressed his disbelief that he had really been hypnotised at all because he had 'not been unconscious but had heard all the suggestions.' It was explained that this was quite natural and that it was the suggestions, not the hypnosis, which would cure him. A week later he reported that he had not touched a drop of drink and had had no desire to do so, much to his amazement and that of his friends.

This was all the more striking as he was actively engaged in the drink trade. Nevertheless he still expressed doubts about whether he had been hypnotised or not. Apparently he and his friends had got together to discuss his remarkable cure, and having seen a stage performance had decided that he could not have been hypnotised as he had not been rendered 'powerless.' A few sessions, however, during which he never achieved anything more than a light trance, were sufficient to produce a complete cure of his alcoholism and he grudgingly admitted that there 'must be something in it.' Other bad habits such as excessive smoking, sex perversions, bed-wetting and nail-biting and blushing will respond equally well.

The patients' behaviour in hypnosis is influenced to a large extent by what they expect. In Mesmer's day nobody considered themselves properly 'influenced' until they had had a convulsion. The fashion changed when the 'sleeping' stage was accidentally discovered because a poor peasant boy who did not know the rules went to 'sleep' instead of having a 'convulsion'!

If the spate of stage exhibitions had continued much longer, no patient would have considered himself hypnotised unless he had been stretched out like a zombie between two chairs and sat upon! It is essential that patients, and indeed the medical profession too, should realise that hypnosis as demonstrated by stage or amateur hypnotists is neither necessary nor desirable for medical purposes. Performers, no matter how well-intentioned they may be, who claim to be furthering the cause of medical science by demonstrating hypnotism, or rather one limited part of it, on the stage or amateur 'clinic' are directly responsible for giving the public a false idea of the subject and do far more harm than good.

Another remark which is quite common is this: 'I am afraid you will be unable to send me to sleep, as I suffer from insomnia and can never sleep properly.' This is based on the popular idea that hypnosis is 'sleep,' and stage and amateur hypnotists without exception further it by ordering their subjects to 'go to sleep,' 'go to sleep.' Most people are astonished to learn that all scientific tests show that the trance is more like the waking state than sleep. For instance, the knee jerk is present in hypnosis but absent or greatly diminished in ordinary sleep. When it is pointed out that the hypnotised person will obey spoken commands, whereas the subject in ordinary sleep takes no notice, most patients are able to appreciate that there is a difference. Further, the phenomena of hypnosis can be developed in the waking state. Everybody is familiar with the test of suggestibility so often presented as 'mass hypnosis' on the stage, where the subjects, although wide awake, are unable to unlock their clasped hands. With explanation and considerable patience, it is usually possible to convince the patient that 'sleep' is not necessary for hypnotic suggestion. Such a condition is illustrated in the case of Mrs. ———. The patient was an elderly widow who had suffered from insomnia for years and was addicted to taking heavy doses of sleeping drugs. The habit had originated apparently during a time of considerable worry and stress when she had to nurse her dying husband under extremely distressing conditions.

Worry over her inability to sleep merely aggravated her condition, and fear as to its eventual consequences caused her great distress. As with all sufferers from insomnia, in whom the mere mention of sleep is enough to keep them wide awake, it was necessary to induce hypnosis without reference to sleep. It was explained that 'sleep' as she understood it was not necessary for hypnosis and that beneficial results would be obtained if she followed certain simple directions. In this way it was possible to induce a light stage of hypnosis and make the appropriate suggestions. Even after the first treatment she reported an improvement, and several sessions were sufficient to free her from the habit of taking drugs and enabled her to sleep naturally. Such a case would never have been able to achieve hypnosis by stage methods with their insistence on 'sleep' and 'deep' hypnosis.

Another idea which patients, and indeed medical men, have is that hypnosis is only useful in the very minor nervous illnesses. A well-known psychiatrist, for instance, states that hypnosis is very difficult and often hopeless in obsessional cases 'because they cannot relax.' Experience has shown that, with the proper technique, obsessional cases respond very well. Almost certainly they will be unlikely to achieve a deep somnambulistic trance at the first session, but as the following case will show, a deep trance is not necessary for cure.

Mrs. ——, a married woman, was obsessed with the fear that she would injure her child. As a result of the worry and anxiety this caused she suffered from severe insomnia and any sleep she did obtain from drugs was disturbed by terrible nightmares. She would awaken screaming and fighting, and eventually became so depressed that she worried about suicide. Hospital treatment and a course of electroshock therapy had failed to relieve her condition.

A careful history at the first session was sufficient to indicate the cause of her fearful obsession. A light trance was induced and the patient given an explanation of her condition. Even after the first treatment she appeared to be relieved, and six sessions were sufficient to remove her fears completely. There has been no relapse over a considerable period of time.

One of the commonest misconceptions is that sex perversions and disorders are too deeply ingrained to respond to hypnosis. Long-standing cases will, of course, require patience and perseverance, but experience has shown that light hypnosis and suggestion can help even severe conditions of this nature.

Consider the case of Mr. ——.

The patient reported that he was obsessed with the idea that he was a homosexual. Inquiry revealed the fact that he had been married and had children but that domestic difficulties had arisen with his wife. As a result of strained feelings between them, sexual relations became very infrequent and he began to suffer from erotic dreams which were based on childish experiences. This caused him to worry and he sought the advice of a psychoanalyst, who, after a period of treatment, told him that he must be homosexual! The patient was greatly distressed and developed severe anxiety symptoms with constant headaches and became generally depressed over his condition and future.

It was quite obvious from the history that the patient had

really been the victim of an unfortunate chain of circumstances. One thing had led to another and developed a bad habit of thinking, until the patient was finally in the grip of a vicious circle.

Owing to his anxiety he proved to be a very difficult subject, but eventually a light trance was induced and explanations and suggestions for cure were given. After six treatments he reported that he felt a new man, had developed normal sexual feelings, and had achieved normal sex relationships with his wife.

Experience has shown that most cases of sexual disorders of all kinds from impotence in men to frigidity in women respond equally well to hypnosis and suggestion.

Patients often ask if hypnosis can help organic disease. The answer to this is difficult, but medical men are beginning to recognise more and more the importance of the mind and its influence on the bodily functions. Everybody knows, for instance, that worry can cause a nervous headache or nervous indigestion. It is not too fantastic to suppose that continued worry and anxiety could be instrumental in causing, say, a duodenal ulcer. The so-called stress diseases—angina pectoris, high blood pressure, asthma and duodenal ulcer—are well known to have a big nervous element. In all, the importance of rest and relaxation is always stressed. Hypnosis can teach the patient to relax, utterly and completely, body and mind, and so must benefit such conditions.

Some apparently organic diseases are often nervous in origin, such as palpitation of the heart.

Mrs. —— complained that she had suffered from severe and continuous palpitation of the heart for several years. Various treatments had been tried and she had been told that it was 'all nerves.' Inquiry revealed that the condition started after she had nursed a relative who died of heart disease. At the time she had been very upset emotionally and had noticed her own heart beating irregularly. The idea crossed her mind that she might have heart disease also. Although the doctor assured her there was nothing organically wrong, she could not get rid of her secret fear, with the result, of course, that the palpitation continued. When seen for the first time she was greatly distressed, and her condition was not helped by the fact that an unqualified hypnotist had attempted to induce hypnosis, without success. After considerable trouble in overcoming her doubts and fears, it was possible to induce a light trance and make the appropriate suggestions. Even after the first session she felt calmer, and after six treatments at weekly intervals was able to report a complete absence of palpitation. (See Illustration 3.)

It is well known that suggestion can influence the heart rate, and in cases where an emotional cause is suspected hypnosis can help a great deal.

It should be realised that hypnotism is not a 'cure-all,' but used in conjunction with other medical treatment in an intelligent fashion it can be of the greatest value in medicine.

If it is to become widely used and of real practical use as a therapeutic measure, it is essential that the popular and widespread but erroneous idea that only deep hypnosis can be effective should be corrected.

Illustration 3

THE INFLUENCE OF HYPNOTIC SUGGESTION ON THE HEART RATE

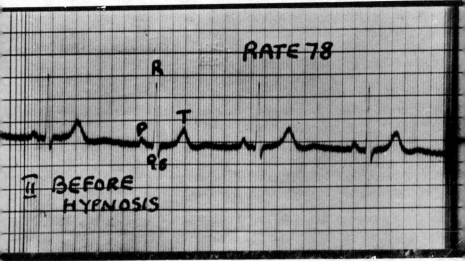

1. Normal Electrocardiogram. This shows a perfectly normal heart capable of standing the test below without fear of damage. This test is an essential precautionary measure.

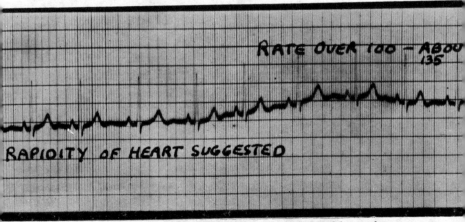

2. Electrocardiogram showing increased rapidity of heart beat as the result of hypnotic suggestion that it should beat quickly.

For further details of this research experiment see Chapter II: 'The Control of the Heart Rate by Hypnotic Suggestion,' by Dr. S. J. Van Pelt. *Experimental Hypnosis* (A Symposium of Articles on Research). Edited by L. M. LeCron. Macmillan & Co., New York, 1952.

(Photograph by courtesy of the *British Journal of Medical Hypnotism*)

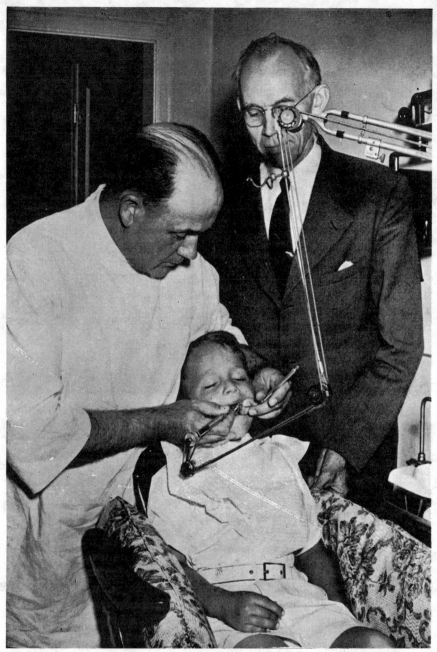

Illustration 4

HYPNOSIS IN DENTISTRY IN U.S.A.

The photograph shows a 4½-year-old boy having his first experience
in a dental chair. Three cavities were prepared and filled during the
half-hour he was in the trance. No sign of discomfort was shown by
the patient. Note the relaxed right hand.

(Photograph by courtesy of the *British Journal of Medical Hypnotism*)

Chapter Four

SOME QUESTIONS PATIENTS ASK ABOUT HYPNOTISM

To ANYONE ENGAGED in the practice of hypnosis for medical purposes, it soon becomes apparent that the patients' pre-conceived ideas play a big part in their attitude to hypnotic treatment, and can, in many cases, influence the result. In this chapter an attempt will be made to answer some of the questions which experience has shown are the ones most frequently asked.

As medical men are naturally more interested in hypnosis as a practical form of therapy than its theoretical niceties, these answers are based on the results of actual personal experience and illustrated by real cases. It is a common, although, of course, not very flattering, experience to hear the patient say: 'Doctor, I've come to you as a last hope.' Inquiry usually reveals the fact that he has put up with years and years of misery and tried all sorts of treatment until 'forced to try hypnotism in desperation.' The reason given is nearly always: 'Well, I thought hypnotism was dangerous and I have always been a bit afraid of it.'

The answer to the question as to whether hypnotism is really dangerous is both 'Yes' and 'No.' Hypnotism can be dangerous, but not in the way so popularly supposed. For some reason the general public seems to be obsessed with the idea of the possibility of sexual seduction or crime under hypnosis. Seduction and various other crimes are taking place day in and day out without any suggestion of hypnosis, but let this be mentioned and certain newspapers feature screaming headlines.

Such a case occurred recently, and many of the newspapers in Great Britain came out with glaring headlines similar to the following:

MRS. X ACCUSES HYPNOTIST!
FORCED HER TO STAY WITH HIM!

They then went on to regale their readers with spicy details of 'Mrs. X,' a young married woman abroad who claimed that a stranger had 'hypnotised' her at a party and forced her to stay with him for two days.

One of the members of our Society—a distinguished medical specialist practising in the country concerned—was asked to investigate the case, and the essential points of his report are as follows: '. . . it has taken me much time to clear up the mentioned affair about the pretended criminal abuse of hypnosis in the case of the young lady, which fortunately has not aroused much attention in this country.

'I telephoned to the newspaper which caused the sensation and found out that the whole matter was a fraud. In reality there had been no talk of hypnosis at all! She had told the story only as an excuse for having betrayed her husband in several cases with a series of different men.'

Such a case is reminiscent of that reported by Bramwell in which he states how he investigated the report that a Swiss medical man had seduced eleven young female patients under hypnosis. Bramwell reports that a copy of the official evidence disclosed the fact that no evidence was found at the trial that hypnotism had been used.

Further, Professor Forel of Zürich stated that 'Dr. M.' had never hypnotised a patient, that the question was not raised at the trial and that nobody had suggested he had used hypnotism! He described 'Dr. M.' as an 'ordinary erotic pig' who had long been known as such and stated that the whole story was an English invention!

Unfortunately these misleading reports can do incalculable harm in undermining the confidence of patients. The case of Mrs. —— well illustrates this.

Sexual Frigidity

This young married woman sought hypnotic treatment as she found it impossible to live a normal married life with her husband. At the preliminary consultation to discuss the case the cause was easily discovered, and arrangements were made for a course of hypnotic treatment. Following the newspaper report already mentioned, she stated that her husband objected to her having hypnosis at all! Fortunately, in this case, it was easy to prove that the whole story was a pure fabrication and the patient was able to have treatment. Even so, it was obvious that the story had made an unfortunate impression and rendered the patient highly nervous and suspicious of hypnotism. After six treatments she reported that she was able to live a normal married life and her husband expressed his gratitude. Such a happy result was, however, nearly rendered impossible by an unintentionally misleading and false story concerning hypnotism.

In another case recently reported, it was alleged that a young girl had been hypnotised by an amateur hypnotist who was accused of committing a serious offence against her. On investigation the magistrates agreed there was no case and the summons was dismissed. Nevertheless 'HYPNOTISM' appeared in thick black letters in the headlines, and no doubt thousands of readers shook their heads and said: 'There you are—I told you so—hypnotism *is* dangerous.'

It is extremely doubtful if anybody could be seduced under hypnosis unless they were of the type that could be seduced much more quickly and easily under normal circumstances. People can be rendered much more helpless and have crimes committed against them by means of alcohol, anaesthetics or certain drugs. Those who desire hypnotic treatment can best safeguard their interests if they have any doubts on the subject by consulting a reputable medical man, who, like his colleagues in other branches of medicine, is bound by strict rules of medical ethics in his conduct towards patients. Such a person is no more likely to attempt to commit a crime against his patient than the family doctor is likely to steal his patient's watch or other valuables!

Apart from the possibilities of seduction some newspapers love to dwell on the criminal aspects of hypnosis. One provincial reporter recently reached the pinnacle of journalistic fame and announced how he had been forced into crime by hypnosis. What was this hideous crime? 'I stole an apple this week,' he confessed!

The country is experiencing the biggest crime wave it has ever known. Murder, robbery with violence and a host of other crimes are an almost daily occurrence. In all of them there is no suggestion of hypnotism, but 'I stole an apple in a hypnotic trance' is worth the headlines! Supposing it were possible to commit crime under hypnosis or persuade another to do it, what are we to do about it? Forbid the practice of hypnotism? Should we forbid the practice of medicine or surgery because deaths have been known to occur even in orthodox practice? Must the use of drugs be forbidden because somebody takes an overdose and commits suicide? Obviously not, but the law does its best to protect the interests of people in these matters. It requires a doctor to put in many years of hard study, pass a stiff examination and to conform to the strictest possible rules of conduct before he is considered competent to treat human beings. The law, however, is an ass in many respects, and it allows any 'quack' in this country, no matter how medically ignorant, to make the most blatant claims. Such people find hypnotism a Godsend and regard it as a sort of back door into medicine without the necessity of doing the hard work which is essential if the practitioner is to be safely entrusted to carry out accurate diagnosis and treatment. Unfortunately it is easy to pick up an elementary knowledge of hypnotism and even obtain a few superficial results in specially selected and highly susceptible subjects.

Hypnotism *can* be dangerous, however, and its real menace lies in its use by medically unqualified people, usually enthusiastic amateurs or stage professionals who dabble in medicine. The case of Miss —— well illustrates the danger of hypnotism when used for apparently harmless demonstration.

This young woman was brought along because for over a year she had been subject to fits of extreme depression with bouts of crying. She suffered from the typical symptoms of anxiety—trembling, sweating, palpitation, difficulty in breathing and intestinal upsets. Concentration was impossible and she stated she could not enjoy anything. She had had all sorts of investigations and psychiatric treatment without any result. Inquiry revealed that just before her illness began, she had taken part in a stage performance. The hypnotist told her that she was very sad and would cry for her mother. This she did very realistically. The audience naturally roared with applause, and, thus encouraged, the hypnotist proceeded to greater efforts. In the rush of the stage performance evidently he had forgotten to remove the original suggestion. As a result the girl

44

began to have (to her) unaccountable fits of deep depression and crying. This worried her, as she thought she must be going mad. As a result, she developed the symptoms of anxiety. These frightened her further, and when nobody could help her by orthodox means she became convinced that her mind had been seriously affected. Naturally she had a great fear of hypnosis and many sessions were necessary before she lost her anxiety. This is by no means an isolated case, and the Society has records of many patients who have suffered severe mental and bodily harm as the results of stage and amateur hypnosis.

Unfortunately, it is not only those who volunteer to go on the stage who can be affected. Even members of the audience watching exhibitions of stage hypnotism can be influenced. One mother wrote concerning her daughter's nervous troubles: '. . . her illness began about two weeks after attending a demonstration of hypnotism by ——, during which she was hypnotised for short spells while in the audience.'

From this it is obvious that the practice of hypnotism for entertainment purposes should be forbidden and its use for medical treatment restricted to those whose recognised qualifications show that they have proved their fitness to diagnose and treat their fellow human beings.

Another question which frequently crops up when explaining the necessity for a properly planned course of treatment is: will it act at once? Again the answer is 'Yes' and 'No.' Patients almost without exception seem to have an idea that hypnosis is simply a matter of being knocked unconscious by some magic process, receiving a suggestion and waking up a different person. This idea arises from the observation of stage and amateur hypnotists, who, of course, work only with specially selected, highly suggestible subjects. A 'good' subject will often accept and carry out a post-hypnotic suggestion at once if so ordered, hence the success of stage performers who find it easy to get their subjects to shout out 'Groundnuts' or some similar thing. It is a different story when one comes to treat highly nervous and anxious people. Generally speaking, nervous cases will need several sessions. This belief that suggestion must work at once or else fail is quite wrong, and can jeopardise the treatment. This is well illustrated in the case of Mr. ——, a young married man, who reported his inability to live a normal married life. He was greatly worried and depressed as his wife threatened a divorce. At the preliminary consultation the cause was easily discovered and it was explained that he would need several treatments. At this he expressed surprise, saying that he thought one treatment would be sufficient. Asked why he thought this, he produced an article from a popular magazine which was alleged to be written by a doctor. Needless to say, his name did not appear in the Medical Directory, and from the subject-matter the article contained it appeared to have been more probably written by the office boy in a moment of mental aberration than by a specialist in hypnosis. All sorts of wonderful cures were performed in this 'doctor's' office, all apparently in the space of five minutes or so! It was explained to the patient that cheap magazines and hack writers had found hypnotism to be a Godsend and that the stories they printed had little or no basis in fact.

Nevertheless, the harm was done. At the second treatment the patient reported that he had been unable to consummate the marriage and expressed his disappointment with hypnosis. He was reminded that he had been warned not to try and assured that the suggestions would act in time. After six sessions he was able to lead a normal life, but his chances of happiness were nearly ruined by a foolish magazine article.

Members of the public should safeguard themselves by consulting the Medical Directory, which is freely available in any public library. If the 'doctor' does not appear in it, his statement concerning hypnosis can be given the attention it deserves.

When explaining to patients that it is the suggestion which will cure them and not the hypnosis, they often ask why suggestion is better under hypnosis than ordinary suggestion?

Now, as we know, even in the waking state, suggestion is very powerful. A single word or phrase can make a person feel happy, sad, angry or afraid and evoke all the bodily symptoms which accompany these feelings. Nevertheless, in the waking state only a fraction of the available 'mind power' is affected by the suggestion. If we consider the brain to contain so many units of 'mind power' we can imagine them jumping about all over the place like a thousand monkeys in a cage. If we then

46

imagine a stream of suggestion going into the brain it will be seen that only a few units will be affected. When, however, all the available mind power is concentrated in the centre by hypnosis, then all the units will receive a dose of suggestion. After the hypnosis, when the mind resumes its waking state, each unit will have a small dose of suggestion. Thus with repetition and proper suggestion it is possible to saturate the whole mind so that the patient thinks as desired. (See Diagram 1.)

The value of hypnotic suggestion is well illustrated in the following cases. A factor which is common to all nervous cases is their inability to relax. In cases such as high blood pressure, insomnia, asthma, and the so-called stress diseases, doctors all tell the patients to 'Relax—take it easy,' but they do not tell them how to do it. If hypnosis did nothing else, it would be of the greatest value in showing the patient how to relax completely, body and mind.

Consider the case of Mr. ——. This patient was a business man in an important position. He complained of high blood pressure, irritability, insomnia, inability to relax or concentrate properly, and 'unpleasant feelings' in the head. His doctor had advised him to 'relax and take it easy,' but he could not do this in spite of taking drugs. After a few sessions he was able to relax and wrote some time later that he was keeping very well. He had had his blood pressure taken by his doctor and it was lower than it had been three months previously. Also he had lost the 'unpleasant feelings' in the head. Hypnosis had demonstrated to the patient that he could relax and enabled him to accept the suggestion 'relax and take it easy' which he had previously been unable to do in his ordinary waking state.

Its value in the treatment of the stress diseases is obvious, and is well illustrated in the case of Mr. ——.

The patient was a very busy professional man who stated that he was unable to relax. Heavy doses of sleeping tablets were necessary to sleep. In a few sessions the patient was taught to relax completely, body and mind. He reported that he was able to send himself to sleep easily and quickly without any drugs, in spite of his busy professional life. He had been told to relax time and time again but could never do it until he tried hypnosis.

Consider the case of Mr. ——. This young man suffered from severe attacks of asthma which had resisted all orthodox methods of treatment. At the preliminary inquiry, the cause was easily discovered. The patient had had several operations and always dreaded the anaesthetic, as he felt as if he were choking. Gradually any anxiety became sufficient to bring on an attack. After several sessions he reported himself free from attacks and was able to sleep peacefully. He had never been able to relax previous to having hypnosis.

With better understanding of the essentially simple and practical nature of medical hypnosis, it is hoped that the public and profession alike will lose their superstitious awe of the subject and make full and early use of this valuable means of medical treatment, rather than regard it as a 'last desperate measure.'

Chapter Five

'3-D' TECHNIQUE IN MEDICAL HYPNOTHERAPY

THERE HAS BEEN much talk about '3-D' or three-dimensional films, the idea behind this development being apparently to bring yet more realism to the cinema screen. Even the old-fashioned black-and-white movies, let alone the coloured variety, have exerted a tremendous influence on our civilisation, and the role they can play in the realms of education and propaganda, besides their primary purpose of entertainment, can hardly be exaggerated. Many people, indeed, consider that films of the harmful variety by glamorising the vicious and degenerate gangster types may have contributed materially to the postwar crime wave. Be that as it may, the influence of pictures and their importance in conveying ideas to the human mind has been known from the earliest times.

'One picture is worth a thousand words' is an old Chinese proverb, and even the primitive cavemen recorded the events of their ordinary everyday lives in their crude but nevertheless highly significant drawings.

The written language itself undoubtedly developed from the picture writing and primitive hieroglyphics of bygone civilisations.

The importance of all this to the hypnotherapist is that pictures can give rise to an idea which in turn gives rise to 'feelings.' These feelings result from the action of the autonomic nervous system, which acts quite automatically, and quite independent of the will, on all the organs and glands of the body in response to impulses set up by the idea. This nervous system, although so incredibly efficient in running the body, is very vulnerable in one respect. It is quite unable to tell the difference between a real thing and an imaginary one. Thus real food can make the mouth water, and the mere thought of imaginary food can do the same thing. Likewise real danger can give rise to the unpleasant feelings of fear, and imaginary danger will do the same. It does not matter what the 'danger' is—one man might be afraid of bankruptcy, while another might fear illness, and yet another might be afraid of ridicule. Whatever the fear may be, unpleasant feelings will result through the action of the autonomic nervous system. From this it will be seen that an idea can produce physical changes in any organ or gland in the body. (See Diagram 2.)

The particular organ, gland or system affected will depend upon the idea aroused, and one of the simplest and most effective methods of arousing an idea is by means of painting a word picture. Thus, if it is desired to make the mouth water— that is, to cause the salivary glands to work—it is only necessary to talk about a 'nice juicy steak' or some other dish which is known to appeal to the patient. It is important, of course, to know exactly what suggestions the patient will accept. A strict vegetarian, for instance, is scarcely likely to respond to the picture of a 'nice, juicy steak' but would probably prefer a vivid description of a delicious 'nut cutlet.' It is strange to note in this connection how often vegetarians seem to like their dishes made up and named as a sort of imitation 'animal' food!

The organ or gland is not influenced by giving it a direct suggestion. The hypnotherapist does not simply say 'Salivary gland—work!' but paints a picture of some food which will appeal to the subject.

Scientific research has shown that hypnotic suggestion can control the blood calcium (Glaser[*]) and the blood sugar (Povorinskij and Finne[†]). Likewise biliary and gastric secretions have been proved to respond to hypnotic suggestion (Langheinrich[‡] and Delhougne and Hansen[§]). Even the heart rate has been controlled (Van Pelt[||]). Yet we still have

[*] Glaser, F., Med. Klin, 1924, 20, 535.

[†] Povorinskij, J. A., and Finne, W. N.: Zeitschrift für die gesamte Neurologie una Psychiatry, 1930, 129, 135.

[‡] Langheinrich, O., 'Psychische Einflüsse auf die Sekretionstätigkeit des Magens und des Diodenume,' Muchen Medizinische Wochenschrift, 1922, 69, 1527.

[§] Delhougne, F., and Hansen, K., 'Die suggestive Beeinflussbarkeit der Magen und Pankreassekretion in der Hypnose,' Deutsches Archiv für Klinische Medizin, 1927, 157, 20.

[||] Van Pelt, S. J., 'The Control of the Heart Rate by Hypnotic Suggestion.' Experimental Hypnosis (a Symposium on Research). Edited by LeCron. Macmillan Publishing Co., New York, 1952. Chapter II.

ignorant sceptics who can see in hypnotism nothing but a music-hall 'stunt.'

Now 'word pictures' are particularly easy to evoke in hypnosis of even the lightest kind and are always much more 'real' or '3-D' in type than those aroused by ordinary suggestion in the waking state.

Indeed in the very deepest stages of hypnosis—somnambulism —it is possible to induce visual hallucinations to such an extent that the subject will 'see' non-existent objects suggested, or will, on the other hand, fail to see real objects if it is suggested that he will not see them.

Visual imagery has been used a great deal in various ways in hypnotherapy—Erickson* has pointed out its value as an induction technique and Wolberg† has described its use in revealing hidden subconscious thoughts by means of fantasy and dream induction.

The writer has found it of the greatest value in the re-education of the patient, which is an essential part of hypnotherapy. In this method, after the cause of the trouble has been discovered and as a part of his re-education, the patient is instructed while under only light hypnosis to 'form a picture' in his mind. He is asked to imagine a cinema screen—nowadays it must be '3-D,' of course!—and to see himself 'just like an actor' on this screen playing a part. He is told that the picture looks 'very real'—'3-D' in fact—and that he can see himself acting and looking the way he really wants to look and act. Various scenes are suggested such as it is known that the patient will have to face in real life. In each he is instructed to see himself—'as in real life'—always succeeding. For instance, the stammerer might be asked to picture himself speaking easily to people, and feeling perfectly at ease. The patient is also instructed how to form these 'success pictures' for himself, and it is stressed that he will only be able to see himself as he wants to be—successful. Since the pictures give rise to the appropriate feelings, it is not long before the patient begins to show the benefit of his private '3-D' film shows. The

* Erickson, M. H., 'Deep Hypnosis and Its Induction.' *Experimental Hypnosis.* Edited by LeCron. Macmillan Publishing Co., New York, 1952. Chapter IV.

† Wolberg, L. R., *Medical Hypnosis.* Grune & Stratton, New York, 1948. Chapter VI, page 148.

following cases are typical examples of the results which can be achieved by this simple method.

Obsessional Neurosis with Asthma and Catarrh

Mr. ——, a middle-aged married man, complained that he was unable to work because in every office the mere presence of a gas or electric fire would cause him such distress that he had to give up the job. He was obsessed with the idea that artificial heating of this kind would cause catarrh and asthma, and spent most of his time examining every nook and cranny to make sure there were no hidden gas or electric fires. After the cause had been discovered and explained, the patient was encouraged to see himself 'in mental pictures' like an actor on the screen working cheerfully under the very conditions of which he complained. After only half a dozen sessions he wrote to say that he had completely lost his fears and had obtained a position.

Alcoholism

Mrs. ——, a widow of forty-five, had been drinking heavily for many years after the death of her husband. As part of her re-education she was encouraged to see herself 'as she really wanted to be.' She was instructed to see herself refusing drink at a party, for instance, and encouraged to visualise herself looking better and enjoying life in various ways as the result of giving up alcohol. After only four treatments the patient had given up alcohol and all her friends remarked how well she looked.

Insomnia and Anxiety

Mr. ——, a middle-aged married man, reported that he was 'going mad with insomnia,' could not concentrate and was losing his memory to such an extent that he could not work. After the cause of his condition had been discovered and explained, he was directed to see himself 'like an actor on the 3-D screen.' As the result of 'playing the part' in his mind's eye of a confident man with no worries who dropped off to sleep the moment his head touched the pillow it was not long before the patient reported himself cured of his trouble and 'sleeping like a baby.'

Stammering

A young man of about twenty-one reported that he was in danger of losing his job because of his nervous stammering. This was especially bad when he had to speak to his boss in the office. The cause was easy enough to discover, but his real improvement started soon after he began his '3-D' exercises—seeing himself like an actor on the screen. He was encouraged to visualise himself speaking easily to the boss even when the latter was in one of his famous tempers. The patient's cure was so striking that the news spread and the boss's own daughter applied for treatment!

Migraine and Stage Fright

Mr. ——, a young professional musician, became so 'worked up' before a concert performance that he almost invariably brought on a severe migraine headache. In many cases this meant losing an important engagement and his career was seriously threatened.

The cause of his anxiety having been discovered, he was encouraged to form 'mental success pictures' and to see himself playing easily and enjoying it, without the slightest anxiety. After a few sessions he reported that he 'felt entirely different' and was able to look forward to engagements with pleasure, instead of anxiety and fear. He improved so much that he was able to undertake a long and strenuous concert tour without the slightest trouble.

These and many similar cases have proved the value of visual imagery in hypnotherapy. On no account, however, should the patient be instructed to 'picture away' his condition until the underlying causative factors have been discovered and dealt with appropriately. With these precautions it is submitted that the '3-D' technique in hypnotherapy can be invaluable.

Chapter Six

SOME DANGERS OF STAGE OR AMATEUR HYPNOTISM

OVER THE LAST few years public attention has been periodically focused on stage or amateur hypnotism, usually as the result of subjects following foolishly given post-hypnotic suggestions. Reports of 'recurrent trances' involving quite often admission to hospital and psychiatric treatment, workers falling 'asleep' in charge of machinery and others behaving foolishly at considerable risk to themselves are common enough. Although Parliament by passing the Hypnotism Act has greatly reduced the activities of professional performers, stage hypnotism is not entirely banned. Furthermore, their amateur counterparts, appearing as lay 'healers' or 'psychologists' (anybody can call himself a 'psychologist' without recognised qualifications!), often give shows disguised as 'lectures' or 'demonstrations.' The dangers outlined here apply just as much to amateur or lay hypnotism as to the out-and-out stage variety.

Stage and lay hypnotists have often indignantly denied (in the face of obvious evidence to the contrary) that any harm could possibly result from exhibitions of stage or amateur hypnosis. Many, indeed, have gone much further and claimed that their performances have enlightened the public and the medical profession as to the value of hypnotism in medicine. Although the danger involved, say, in the case of a car driver falling into a trance ('asleep'), as the result of hearing a particular tune played on the car radio, in response to a carelessly worded post-hypnotic suggestion is perfectly clear, there are other equally serious although not so obvious dangers in stage or lay hypnotism which, it is hoped, this chapter will reveal.

How Stage or Amateur Hypnotists Work

Before details of their methods can be appreciated, it is necessary to know something of hypnotism, for even an elementary knowledge of the subject will be sufficient to 'debunk' the fantastic claims of the so-called 'experts,' who rely upon the ignorance and superstition of the majority of the public, and many of the medical profession, concerning hypnosis. Briefly, hypnotism is the science and art of inducing a trance state known as hypnosis. It has nothing to do with sleep, and all scientific tests show that it is more like the waking state than ordinary sleep. The condition may be induced by an operator or the subject himself without even any mention of sleep. The degree of trance varies from very light to the very deep somnambulistic state. While 95 per cent of people can be hypnotised to one degree or another, only about 25 per cent can be regarded as potential somnambulists. Various phenomena can be observed in the trance, the chief ones being increased suggestibility, rapport (subject is in sympathy with and responds to the hypnotist only), sensory changes (anaesthesia, etc.), muscular changes (rigidity, paralysis, etc.), automatic writing (subconscious writing), age regression (the mind can return to specified levels of early life), positive and negative hallucinations of all the senses (the subject can 'see,' 'feel,' 'hear,' 'taste' or 'smell' non-existent things as ordered, or fail to notice real things if told to ignore them), psychosomatic phenomena (abnormal control over bodily organs by the mind), post-hypnotic suggestions (orders given during trance are carried out later at a specified time or place in the waking state), and amnesia (loss of memory for events in the trance or anything else ordered by the operator).

Even in the lightest stage of hypnosis, suggestibility is greatly increased, and with proper technique valuable medical work can be carried out, but the more spectacular, bizarre phenomena can be obtained only in the deep (somnambulistic) state. This is the only state of any use to the stage hypnotist. Contrary to what is generally believed, the hypnotist has no 'power' whatsoever—the 'power' used is really the subject's own imagination. The hypnotist merely persuades him to use his imagination to its fullest extent by suggestion and it 'works' on the simple principle that suggestion of food, for instance, to a hungry person can make the mouth water.

The stage or amateur hypnotist deliberately selects highly suggestible people by means of very simple tests. A favourite one is to ask members of the audience to clasp their hands together and think (or imagine) they are 'locked.' Obviously those who cannot undo their hands when challenged are highly suggestible and will make good subjects.

As about 25 per cent of the population fall into this class, it is quite simple for stage hypnotists to be certain of obtaining sufficient 'easy' subjects in any large audience to give a demonstration. Such people will go into a deep trance very quickly and easily by almost any method, and even the veriest amateur could hypnotise them.

Far from being the great 'experts' their publicity managers claim them to be, stage hypnotists are required to exhibit the very minimum of hypnotic ability on the easiest of subjects under the most favourable conditions. To paraphrase a well-known quotation, one might well say: 'What can they know of hypnotism who only stage hypnotism know?' Indeed, stage hypnotists may be regarded as the veriest amateurs in the hypnotic sense whose success depends upon a flair for showmanship and a good publicity agent.

The Deception of Stage or Amateur Hypnotism Gives an Entirely Wrong Impression of the Subject

Stage or amateur hypnotists seldom, if ever, bother to explain that they are demonstrating only a small fraction of hypnotism—the induction and phenomena of a deep trance in specially selected, highly suggestible subjects. The impression is given that all people can be hypnotised as on the stage. This is definitely not so, particularly in the case of nervous and highly anxious persons who are the very ones to whom medical (not stage) hypnosis can bring most benefit. Nevertheless these nervous and anxious people, who would never have the 'nerve to go on the stage as volunteers or the imagination to 'lock their hands' or the ability to concentrate on the hypnotist's suggestions, all expect to perform like stage subjects when seeking medical hypnosis.

Invariably they expect to be forced to 'go under' by the

'power' of the hypnotist, and be made to give up their symptoms while 'knowing nothing about it.'

Disappointment at their failure to be 'deeply hypnotised' (like the subjects on the stage or at demonstrations) may easily prevent them obtaining the relief they seek, when a proper understanding of the subject would enable them to benefit from light to medium hypnosis, which is often quite sufficient for medical purposes.

As we have seen, there are always enough highly suggestible people in any large audience to guarantee 'good subjects' for a show, but it is not unknown for stage or amateur hypnotists to make doubly sure by having a few 'trained subjects' planted in the audience. Such people 'go to sleep' almost instantly at any prearranged signal, and so set an example to others.

Some stage hypnotists do not hesitate to use a dangerous ju-jitsu wrestling trick (pressure on the neck) to render a 'refractory' subject unconscious and apparently hypnotised.

Stage or Amateur Hypnotism is Exactly the Wrong Type for Medical Purposes

First of all it is quite obvious that hypnotism would be of little use in medicine if doctors (like stage hypnotists) could select only highly suggestible, easy patients for treatment. Nervous and anxious patients, who need hypnosis most, seldom make 'good subjects' and usually have to be patiently trained to achieve sufficient hypnosis for medical purposes.

Secondly, stage hypnotism is strongly authoritarian, and more often than not it is based on fear. It demands that the subject should 'do this or that.' When this method is applied for medical purposes, the patient is ordered to give up his symptoms—'give up smoking,' 'stop drinking alcohol,' 'stop biting your nails,' etc. It treats symptoms only. Excessive smoking, drinking and other neurotic symptoms from nail-biting to insomnia are only indications of underlying nervous disorder. It is useless and harmful to attempt merely to suppress the symptoms without treating the cause. If one symptom is suppressed, another will most probably take its place, and it is the wrong method of using hypnotism (as demonstrated by stage and amateur hypnotists) which has given the subject a bad name and given rise to the old bogy, 'the results of hypnotism are only temporary.'

Hypnotism should not be blamed simply because it is used wrongly. Even the results of dentistry would be 'temporary' were the dentist foolish enough merely to remove the pain of a decayed tooth with an injection instead of treating the root of the trouble. Stage and lay hypnotists are forced to treat symptoms only, for it is quite obvious that they can have no real medical or psychological training.

'Reading a book on psychology' no more fits a person to treat the mind than reading a book on surgery would make him a surgeon! The mind controls the body, and anybody who sets out to treat either should be properly qualified by recognised training and experience. It is highly unlikely that stage or lay hypnotists could even enumerate the symptoms of the complaints they profess to treat, let alone give a differential diagnosis.

A 'headache,' for instance, may be simple, due to worry, blood pressure, kidney disease or a cerebral tumour, not to mention a hundred other possible causes. No layman could honestly claim to diagnose accurately between the various conditions, yet stage hypnotists dabbling in medicine will cheerfully 'order' the headache to go, without any idea of treating the cause.

Stage and amateur hypnotism and the method it advocates (suppression of symptoms only) is more likely to cause neurosis than cure it! In many cases the patient's symptom is a form of protection, and if forced to give it up before the underlying condition has been recognised and treated he may be unable to face life without it and even suicide may result.

Claims of Co-operation with Doctors

Stage and lay hypnotists who dabble in medicine frequently claim that they treat only cases which have been diagnosed by a doctor. However, co-operation between a doctor who knows nothing of hypnotism and a layman who knows nothing of medicine is a supreme example of the blind leading the blind. Many complaints have an insidious onset, and there may be little to show in the early stages. An early symptom of pulmonary tuberculosis, for instance, may be simply an increased tiredness or loss of energy. An ordinary clinical examination might reveal nothing, and if the general practitioner then turned the case over to a lay hypnotist to treat as a case of 'nervous exhaustion' the latter would undoubtedly try to stimulate the patient to greater efforts, probably by the only method he would know—direct suggestion.

Developing symptoms, which any doctor keeping the patient under observation would recognise, might easily be disguised or hidden by the hypnosis, so that the disease could progress unsuspected or unchecked until a late stage had been reached.

For medical purposes the obvious person to carry out treatment by hypnosis is a properly qualified doctor who understands both medicine and hypnosis—and the word 'medicine' is used in its widest sense and includes a knowledge of psychology, for the mind and body are one. It has been suggested by unthinking people that doctors should employ lay hypnotists as medical auxiliaries in the same way as masseurs or physiotherapists. The difference, however, is that with the hypnotist the treatment is entirely in his hands. The General Medical Council has recognised this, and, as stated in the *British Medical Journal*, co-operation between a doctor and a lay hypnotist has been declared unethical.

Claims to 'Teach the Doctors' Medical Hypnosis

Stage and lay hypnotists seldom fail to seek publicity by claiming that they are promoting the cause of medical hypnotism and 'teaching the doctors.' Were any doctor foolish enough to seek instruction from one of these people, what could he learn? At the most, simply how to induce a state of deep trance in a specially selected, highly suggestible subject. He could not learn medical hypnosis, for medical hypnosis can no more be demonstrated on the stage than psychoanalysis.

There are many thousands of real scientific works on hypnotism—a recent book, for instance, has a bibliography of fifty pages!—and all of them have been written by doctors and properly qualified scientific workers. The great 'experts' of the stage and lay healers are conspicuous by their absence in the scientific literature on hypnosis, and the 'important researches' they claim to carry out are somehow not included in the scientific records. It is only necessary to study the history of the subject to find a long list of properly qualified medical men such as Mesmer, Braid, Elliotson, Esdaile, Liébeault, Bernheim, Bramwell among the early pioneers.

It must be realised that mere ability to induce hypnosis in an easy, susceptible subject (which anybody can acquire) is *not* sufficient for medical purposes and that enthusiasm, no matter how well meant, is *not* an efficient substitute for lack of proper medical knowledge.

A favourite publicity stunt for stage or amateur hypnotists is to give a demonstration at some hospital, nursing or medical centre and then claim that they are 'teaching the doctors the medical uses of hypnosis.' Such demonstrations may be more in the nature of an entertainment, much as other showmen give for charity, and although they might show the doctors the stage method of hypnosis it is quite certain that they do *not* demonstrate how hypnosis should really be used in medicine. How can they, having had no real (as opposed to professed) medical training?

It would be a sad thing for nervous and anxious patients were doctors foolish enough to practise the crude methods of the stage or amateur hypnotists upon them.

Risks of Mental and Physical Harm from Stage and Amateur Hypnosis

The only people who are suitable for stage demonstrations of hypnotism are the highly suggestible ones who are capable of entering a deep trance very quickly and easily. Such people may easily suffer considerable mental and physical harm, as suggestions can have very powerful effects upon them. Suggestions on the stage are almost invariably aimed at making the subject appear ridiculous and amusing the audience.

As a result we get foolish suggestions such as 'You are very, very sad; cry, cry hard for your mother,' etc., etc., or more degrading ones such as 'Now you are drunk.' Apparently superficial suggestions can have far-reaching and unforeseen effects, as a study of the cases mentioned later on will reveal.

Definite Mental Harm May Result

The subject may begin to have unpleasant feelings or re-current trances as the result of foolish or carelessly given suggestions. As a result of these apparently inexplicable happenings, the person begins to fear damage to the mind and in an emotional panic literally hypnotises himself. Fear and anxiety create more symptoms and so set up a vicious circle which may lead to serious mental trouble (see cases).

Physical Harm May Easily Result

The subject may 'fall asleep' at some prearranged signal as the result of a post-hypnotic suggestion, and it needs little imagination to see how a serious accident could easily result, particularly if the subject happened to be an air pilot, a bus driver or a motorist.

Physical harm could also result in another way. The subject may be called upon to perform feats which are really undesirable for physical reasons and which may be dangerous to him. For example, a favourite trick is to render the subject quite rigid and have one or two people stand upon him. Injury could easily result in certain cases. No proper tests are ever made beforehand in a stage show to ascertain the patient's fitness for such feats—indeed the stage hypnotist would not even know *how* to test a subject medically. Another trick is to make the subject's heart beat faster than usual, and this could easily cause serious harm to a patient with a weak heart. (See Illustration 3, and note precautions taken to test heart first.)

How Stage and Amateur Hypnotists Continue to Mislead the Public with Impunity

First of all they can, as professional showmen or lay healers unhandicapped by any medical etiquette, advertise both directly and indirectly as much as they like, making the most blatant and extravagant claims without much fear of successful contradiction. Unfortunately, the public craves sensation, and, with the exception of the more responsible papers, the Press is only too anxious to pander to their craving. Anybody who can give a public show or produce a new 'stunt' becomes an 'expert' and his sensational pronouncements are much more acceptable than the cold scientific truth. 'Falsehood is half-way round the world before Truth has got its boots on,' and even if their inaccurate statements are corrected by some qualified person, it is exceptional for the truth to get more than a line or two in some obscure position.

Again the law of this country which requires a dentist to be properly qualified allows anybody to dabble in medicine with impunity. Further, the victims of these stage hypnotists have no real redress in law, in addition to which they are more often than not afraid of further publicity, for nobody likes to have it blazoned abroad that he has been in a mental home. Recently a doctor wrote to say that both he and the father of a young woman, who had suffered considerable mental harm after being hypnotised on the stage, were in full agreement with any attempt to ban exhibitions of stage hypnotism.

Apart from ethical reasons he could not, however, bring the case to the notice of the public because two years after the original hypnosis the patient's mental health was still in the balance and no risks could be taken which might cause her further anxiety and jeopardise her recovery. Thus the victims have to suffer in silence while the stage or lay hypnotists obtain bigger and better advertisements in the news-papers by blandly announcing 'there is no danger in stage hypnotism.'

Typical Cases Illustrating the Dangers of Stage Hypnotism

Mr. ——, a middle-aged man, wrote to a stage hypnotist who attempted to cure him of the smoking habit. The hypnotist had evidently 'read a book' on psychology and apparently attempted some sort of hypnoanalysis. When he suggested that 'all his worries and depressions would come to the surface' the patient became greatly alarmed and 'woke up.' He began to suffer from fits of depression and developed considerable anxiety concerning his state of mind. Much treatment was necessary before his fears could be allayed, and this case illustrates the dangers of amateurs playing with hypnoanalysis.

Mr. ——, a young man, applied for treatment, complaining of nervousness with severe anxiety attacks, lack of confidence and inability to concentrate. It appeared that he had responded to an advertisement by a hypnotist who wanted to 'train good subjects' for demonstrating. The patient had been unable to pass all the tests required of a 'stooge,' but, as the result of trying to carry out various foolish and conflicting suggestions, had developed a real neurosis. Naturally, his unfortunate experience with hypnosis made treatment very difficult, and much patient effort was required to re-educate his mind.

Mr. ——, a young man, had been in the habit of volunteering as a subject for stage hypnotism by various performers. He complained of lack of energy, inability to concentrate on his work and general nervous anxiety. Investigation revealed that his confused condition was obviously due to various conflicting suggestions which had been put into his mind by successive hypnotists, and much treatment was required to restore him to normal.

Miss ——, a young single woman, suffered from 'nervous palpitation.' She sought treatment from a stage hypnotist who dabbled in 'healing.' He promptly diagnosed 'heart trouble,' which frightened her more than ever, and endeavoured to cure it by the naïve method of 'telling the heart to beat quietly.' Needless to say he did not succeed, and the patient developed a severe state of anxiety neurosis concerning her 'incurable heart condition' and much treatment was required to ease her mind.

Mere Spectators Can be Affected by Stage Hypnotism

Unfortunately, it is not only those who volunteer to go on the stage who can be affected. Even members of the audience watching exhibitions of stage or amateur hypnotism can be influenced, for it should be remembered that approximately 25 per cent of people are highly suggestible and are capable of going into a deep trance.

This fact has been recognised by the British Broadcasting Corporation and Television Service, who have refrained from broadcasting performances of stage hypnotism for fear of possible dangerous complications.

One mother wrote concerning her daughter's nervous trouble—'her illness began about two weeks after attending a demonstration by —— during which she was hypnotised for short spells while in the audience.'

Another danger is that people who see demonstrations of hypnotism are very apt to 'have a go' at it themselves. One soldier after a demonstration attempted to hypnotise himself and finished up by being awarded a disability pension for neurosis!

Lack of space does not permit mention of further cases, but enough has been said to make it quite obvious that stage and amateur hypnotism is highly undesirable from many points of view and fraught with potential danger for all, particularly the more suggestible, who take part in or witness these performances.

Nobody in his sane senses would suggest that showmen or laymen should be allowed to demonstrate how they could remove pain by injecting a drug such as morphia. Hypnotism in the wrong hands is just as dangerous and should be fully controlled by law, as it is in most civilised countries abroad. The proper place for hypnotism is in the consulting room of a qualified medical man and it is no more suitable for the stage than any other branch of medicine.

Chapter Seven

HYPNOTHERAPY AND HOW TO SAVE THE COUNTRY'S HEALTH BILL

FROM CASE RECORDS available it is quite certain that modern hypnotherapy could save this country many millions of pounds annually. The Minister of Health has recently stressed that the Exchequer could not be expected to continue paying £40 million a year for drugs prescribed by general practitioners unless they were in fact essential for the proper treatment of patients.

The *British Medical Journal* (20 June, 1953) states: 'Every practising doctor knows that the ingredients of a placebo medicine will do little if anything to readjust a patient's disordered physiology; but he knows, too, that if the patient has a firm belief that he or she will benefit from such and such a remedy then some benefit will be experienced. For the patient there is much "magic" in a bottle of medicine, and in this respect the sick Briton is as primitive in his reactions as the sick savage.'

In addition, a well-known psychiatrist has stated: 'It is safe to say that approximately half the average doctor's practice is concerned with psychoneurosis in one form or another.'

Thus we have the fantastic situation whereby millions of pounds' worth of unnecessary medicine—just 'coloured water' —is being poured down the throats of millions of people annually in what really amounts to extremely crude and unscientific efforts to cure them by suggestion!

When such methods fail, as they are frequently bound to do, patients often embark upon a long series of expensive investigations and costly medical or even surgical treatments.

If their symptoms persist, many patients find their way to the psychiatric clinic. Here, as psychoanalysis (which may take years) is too time-consuming for busy hospital practice, they are more likely than not to receive a course of electro-shock treatment or be recommended for a brain operation such as leucotomy.

It is not denied that there *may* be a place for such drastic treatments in dealing with some cases, but it is maintained that a simple, safe and scientific treatment such as hypnotherapy, if employed early, would prevent the majority of nervous cases from ever reaching the serious stage where such procedures need even be considered.

Very often, the starting-point of the patient's trouble is some emotional upset which causes physical symptoms through the nervous system. Worry over these symptoms merely aggravates them, and so creates a vicious circle. (See Diagram 3.) Indigestion due to worry is not going to be cured by diet or alkalis or even operations.

The only scientific cure is to go right to the root of the trouble and remove the cause of the worry. And hypnotherapy is the ideal method of choice for this.

The following case, typical of reports reaching the society, for instance, indicates the value of hypnotherapy.

'Mrs. —— was sent for treatment because she was emotionally "dead" and "unable to think, decide or take any interest in anything." The hospital report showed that she had been ill for over two years, and that psychotherapy, including prolonged narcosis, had produced no improvement. She had been advised "to live apart from her husband for a year or two" until she could decide about continuing her marriage.

'Hypnotherapy, however, enabled her to make up her mind in a matter of weeks. She did not leave her husband. Indeed, she made a success of her marriage and was soon quite happily engaged bringing up a family!'

Another typical case in which hypnotherapy was able to help was that of Mrs. ——.

'This young married woman was referred for hypnotherapy "as a last resort." For over five years she had been prostrate with nervous tension. And all usual treatment with tonics, injections, sleeping tablets and other drugs had failed to relieve the condition. She suffered from migraine-like headaches, insomnia and frequent attacks of "panic." It was impossible for her to go out on her own, to go shopping or visit cinemas or theatres, even with her husband.

'It was soon revealed that she was afraid of losing her husband, since her discovery that he had been unfaithful on one occasion.

'A short course of hypnotherapy enabled her to adjust her attitude, and relaxation dispelled the nervous tension which had been wearing her out.'

It is suggested that the Ministry of Health should support an Institute of Hypnotherapy to carry out teaching, clinical and research work on this important branch of medical treatment.

It is quite certain that the establishment of such an institute would justify its existence within a very few years by reducing the cost of the Health Service, easing the pressure on mental homes and, above all, promoting the welfare and happiness of patients.

It is a very welcome sign that the importance of hypnotherapy has been recognised by the World Health Organisation, which has included the *British Journal of Medical Hypnotism* in its official publication *World Medical Periodicals*.

Is it too much to hope that we shall soon see the Ministry of Health following this good example and embarking upon a constructive programme designed to bring the benefits of hypnotherapy within the reach of all?

Chapter Eight

HYPNOSIS AND ANXIETY

AT A TIME when the National Health Service is strained to breaking point both from lack of funds and shortage of hospital beds, and doctors' surgeries are filled to overflowing, it is more important than ever to realise the part played by anxiety in the production of illness.

This is even more essential when it is considered how many gallons of medicine were poured down the throats of patients more than half of whom had no real need of drugs at all and were suffering merely from the effects of anxiety.

It was recently reported that an official of the Health Ministry had appealed to the public to avoid wasting the time of doctors in unnecessary calls and had complained of the 'appalling national bottle habit.'

Statistics were given showing that 202 million prescriptions had been issued in 1949, which, allowing for a population of 45 millions, worked out at nearly five each for every man, woman and child in the country! In 1950 the figure had risen to 218 millions, and this did not include medicine prescribed during the influenza epidemic!

The expense involved in providing unwanted spectacles and other appliances, with needless investigations such as X-rays, electrocardiograms and pathological tests, together with the famous 'bottle of medicine' pales into insignificance when the economic loss to the country resulting from the effects of anxiety is considered.

It is no exaggeration to say that much of the absenteeism and industrial strife so prevalent today is due to anxiety, and, as this condition is no respecter of persons, it makes itself felt among all classes of society from bus conductors to Cabinet Ministers.

Although it is probably quite true to say that anxiety has

always existed, there is no doubt that the stresses and strains of modern conditions have brought about an enormous increase in the incidence of this complaint, so that it bids fair to become the outstanding and most prevalent illness of the twentieth century.

Unfortunately, as will be seen later, the symptoms resulting from anxiety often mimic those of real organic disease, and, until recently, the importance of the mental element has been little realised. The tendency has always been to give the patient a 'bottle of medicine,' and every doctor knows quite well that very often a bottle of coloured water or some equally chemically and therapeutically inert substance has 'worked wonders.'

However, for every success resulting from such crude 'hit or miss' method of suggestion, there are literally hundreds of people who have had their neuroses firmly fixed and even aggravated by useless 'bottles of medicine' and needless investigations.

Those who hold themselves up as 'champions of the people' and base their claims to fame on the number of bottles of 'free medicine' they have caused to be poured down the throats of their supporters would be well advised to consider this fact very carefully.

How then does anxiety show itself?

Typically the patient is subject to attacks of panic for apparently no reason at all. There may be periods of complete freedom in the earlier stages but gradually the patient becomes more and more subject to vague fears with irritability and depression.

Physical symptoms such as palpitations, breathlessness, headache, trembling, sweating, intestinal or bladder upsets are very common and cause great distress. Insomnia is nearly always present and worries the patient, while failing memory and loss of the power of concentration make it more and more difficult for the patient to cope with his work. Inability to relax and excessive 'tension' are common complaints.

What then is the cause of this anxiety?

Everyone is familiar with certain circumstances which have on occasion given rise to worry and some anxiety. There are few people who have not experienced feelings of fear on occasion. However, in such cases the cause of the worry or fear is usually very obvious and when removed the unpleasant feelings have disappeared.

The patient suffering from anxiety does not recognise the cause of his fear and feels quite helpless as a result. Typically such a patient will complain 'I have such terrific feelings of panic,' but when asked what it is he fears he will reply: 'I don't know.' This is generally considered to be due to the fact that there is a 'subconscious conflict' between impulses which the patient has found so fearful that he has had to 'repress' them. Based on practical experience, the writer considers that the condition may be best explained by likening the mind to a piece of elastic. (See Diagram 4.) Stretching the elastic by pulling in opposite directions creates tension. Similarly if the mind is 'stretched' or 'pulled apart' or 'strained' by two opposing ideas, then terrific tension will be developed. The energy resulting from this tension upsets the autonomic nervous system and causes unpleasant physical symptoms. (See Diagram 2.) These symptoms, such as palpitation, shortness of breath, trembling, sweating, and others of an equally distressing nature, give rise to fear. This fear in turn gives rise to more symptoms and so a vicious circle is established. (See Diagram 3.) The patient becomes afraid of the symptoms of fear and in the process of concentrating on these forgets the original cause of the trouble.

It is commonly believed that years of analysis are required to bring to light these 'deeply buried conflicts,' but in the writer's experience it has been found relatively simple to discover these conflicting and opposing ideas by taking a careful history in the waking state without any deep 'subconscious probing' or prolonged analysis. A few adroit questions soon bring to light the salient facts, and patients are often amazed as the interview proceeds to find themselves remembering details of significant incidents which they thought they had forgotten.

After all, Bernheim was able to recall lost memories by persistent questioning in the waking state, and it was Freud's observation of this fact which eventually led to psychoanalysis.

In nearly every case it has been found that, although many would deny it at first, the patients, from inability to understand

HOW TENSION CAUSES UNPLEASANT SYMPTOMS
AND THE DEVELOPMENT OF A VICIOUS CIRCLE

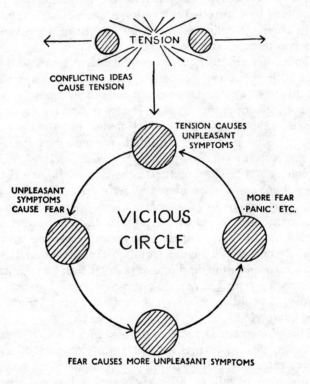

Diagram 4

(Courtesy of the *British Journal of Medical Hypnotism*)

the cause of their condition, have finally developed the greatest fear of all—the fear that there was 'something wrong with their minds.'

Treatment has been aimed at discovering the cause of the conflict, explaining it to the patients, first in the waking state and then under hypnosis, demonstrating their ability to dispel symptoms by controlled relaxation and instilling confidence in their ability to follow a 'one way' course of approved action which eliminates any 'conflicts.'

Before describing typical cases, it might be as well to consider a few reasons why anxiety is becoming so prevalent in the modern world. Depending as it does upon a 'conflict' between two opposing ideas, it is easy to find conditions in our present state of civilisation which favour its growth. For years now it has been scarcely possible to open a newspaper without being confronted with alarming headlines such as 'Will there be war or not?' The unsettled condition of the world today is bad enough, and when presented sensationally day after day it is quite sufficient to have a bad effect on suggestible people. This trend is reflected in the popular taste for entertainment, so that we find the cinema and theatre revelling in 'psychological' themes portraying 'conflicts' in the mind. Even the radio is not immune, and in one popular serial which has been running for years the central character is daily presented with a difficult problem to which she seldom fails to respond with 'I'm so worried.'

This phrase enters more and more into the conversation of everyday life and betrays the uncertainty of mind which forms a favourable breeding-ground for anxiety. Again there has been a distinct falling off in the moral values and the moral fibre of the people in general. There is no longer the clear-cut distinction between right and wrong, and for many people there is no longer any real ideal or guiding principle. As a result, when something important comes up, they are uncertain what to do and waver first one way and then the other and finally develop anxiety.

Personal relationships naturally play an important part, and under modern conditions of housing, or rather lack of it, people whose personalities clash are often thrown together, and the conflicting feelings aroused predispose strongly to anxiety.

In particular this is noticeable where people have to live with their 'in-laws.' The old 'mother-in-law' joke is a favourite one of the music-halls, but consideration of some of the following cases will show that the 'in-law' problem is a real one and a fertile cause of anxiety neurosis under modern conditions. The following cases are all listed under their presenting symptoms, but, as will be seen, were all cases of anxiety neurosis which responded favourably to medical hypnotism.

Insomnia

Mrs. ——, a young married woman, complained of intractable insomnia of several years' duration. She complained that she was 'going mad' for want of sleep and suffered from violent attacks of panic for no reason that she could see. Her doctor had given her very heavy doses of sleeping drugs, with little or no effect. A simple history showed that she lived with her mother-in-law, whom she disliked intensely. The thought had come into her head that she would be unable to stand living with her and that she might 'run away.' This she knew would break up her marriage. These conflicting ideas naturally caused worry and insomnia. Somebody told her she would go mad if she didn't sleep properly. She worried over this so much that soon even sleeping drugs could not help. This convinced her she must be 'going mad' and gave rise to feelings of panic. These feelings terrified her even more and gave rise to a vicious circle. Being absorbed in her unpleasant feelings, she had lost sight of the original simple cause. Explanation and reassurance with a few sessions of hypnosis enabled her to see things in their true light, removed her fears and allowed her to sleep naturally. Incidentally, she developed sufficient confidence to explain matters to her husband and solved the problem of her mother-in-law by finding somewhere else to live.

Asthma

Mrs. ——, an elderly woman, reported with a complaint of severe asthma for over ten years. The patient suffered especially badly at night so that sleep was greatly disturbed. She was terrified of her condition and showed all the symptoms of fear. Ordinary medical treatment had been unable to help. A simple history revealed the fact that the patient greatly resented the behaviour of her son-in-law, who had treated her daughter very badly. The thought crossed her mind 'I'd like to kill him.' Naturally she did not attempt such a thing, but the idea frightened her, and the conflict in her mind generated so much tension that her nervous system was upset, and she began to suffer from asthma. Fear of the distressing symptoms caused more anxiety, with symptoms of panic, so that a vicious circle was established. The patient in her distress had long forgotten the original cause, but a few simple questions soon brought the facts to light. A course of hypnotic treatment extending over half a dozen sessions enabled her to relax and dispel her nervous tension, with consequent disappearance of the asthma and panic attacks.

Migraine

Mrs. —— complained of frequent attacks of migraine extending over many years, together with feelings of panic. Panic attacks were especially likely to occur if she attempted to go anywhere alone. Investigation revealed the fact that she bitterly resented the behaviour of her sister-in-law, with whom she had to live. This was aggravated by the fact that her husband was inclined to take his sister's part in any argument. The patient admitted that the thought had entered her head that she would like to 'run away from it all.' This terrified her, as she loved her husband. The conflict had given rise to tension, which expressed itself as migraine and panic attacks. Fear of these symptoms set up a vicious circle and the patient had lost sight of the original cause of her trouble until it was uncovered by a few simple questions. Several hypnotic sessions enabled her to relax and adopt a more reasonable attitude towards the differences with her sister-in-law, as a result of which she reported the complete cessation of her migraine and panic attacks.

Alcoholism

Mr. —— complained of inability to resist taking excessive quantities of alcohol. The condition had become steadily worse over a number of years and threatened to lose him his position. He stated that he did not know why he drank. Inquiry revealed that he 'could not stand' his mother-in-law, who lived with him. She had had a habit of criticising him and he had refrained from saying what he wanted to say for his wife's sake. He stated that he had noticed himself getting tense and irritable and had first begun to have mild attacks of panic shortly after his mother-in-law had first come to live with them. He freely admitted that he had often felt like 'clearing out,' and would have done so had it not been for the fact that he was deeply in love with his wife. These conflicting ideas set up considerable tension and to relieve this he had taken alcohol. This had resulted in further criticism from his mother-in-law and more resentment on his part. Thus a vicious circle was set up and the patient had to resort to ever-increasing doses of alcohol. When he noticed this, he developed a fear of becoming an alcoholic. His worst fears were realised when he found he could not stop drinking, although he had long forgotten the original cause of his trouble. He was shown that it was quite possible to relax and calm his nerves naturally by means of hypnosis and so render himself independent of alcohol. The patient rapidly developed confidence in himself and was able to give up drink. Furthermore he was able to adopt a more 'don't care' attitude towards his mother-in-law and stated later that her criticisms now just 'bounced off him like water off a duck's back.'

These cases are typical of the wide variety of conditions the basic cause of which is anxiety. More and more the influence of the mind in producing physical illness is being recognised.

Recently in a report on the results of a four-year investigation, the British Medical Association is quoted as saying 'the patient aches in his limbs because, in fact, he aches in his mind.' The pains of the 'chronic rheumatic' it was considered may be due to 'emotional stress' or neurosis.

Over a period of four years, 109 cases were investigated, and although all complained of severe pain, X-ray and pathological investigations revealed no evidence of active rheumatic disease. In 79 per cent there was evidence of neurosis, and half the cases showed anxiety state, usually linked with considerable tension. It was stated that frustration and resentment in a disturbing environmental situation were common. Now that the overwhelming weight of evidence has shown quite clearly the part played by anxiety in producing illness of all kinds, we may hope that the quickest and most effective method of dealing with the problem will receive official approval on a wider scale and medical hypnosis will come into its own. Hypnosis cannot, of course, eliminate the possibility of troublesome relatives, personal misfortunes or world wars, but it can enable people to face up to such problems as are likely to beset them in this modern world instead of running in panic to doctors for pills and potions to subdue their anxiety. It is to be hoped that in future, as this fact is realised more and more, cases will be referred for medical hypnosis first instead of as a 'last resort' when the neurosis has become firmly fixed by the 'bottle of medicine' technique, and then it may be confidently expected that results will be even more striking than those obtained at present.

Chapter Nine

ASTHMA? IS THERE ANY SUCH DISEASE?

At FIRST SIGHT the title of this chapter may appear a little strange when it is remembered that all over the country doctors are frequently called upon, both by day and night, to relieve the sufferings of distressed patients with injections of adrenalin or other powerful drugs. When practically every medical journal, daily newspaper and magazine carries an advertisement for 'So-and-so's Asthma Cure,' and chemists' windows are tastefully decorated with gaily labelled bottles of medicine all guaranteed to relieve the anguish of the asthmatic, one might well be excused for displaying a little scepticism in accepting any statement which suggests that asthma as a disease does not exist!

To the harassed sufferer, anxiously sniffing at his inhaler with the latest anti-spasmodic compound, the suggestion must appear wellnigh incredible. Let it be made quite clear that by the term 'asthma' in this article is meant the ordinary common type of the spasmodic variety, and that the rarer conditions such as cardiac and renal asthma are not included.

How, it may be asked, can there be any doubt about the existence of asthma when it would be difficult indeed to find anybody who did not either have a relative who suffered from the complaint or know of a friend or acquaintance similarly afflicted? Again, to simplify matters, let it be stated that it is not disputed that a condition known as asthma does occur. What is denied is that it is a disease. In fact this article puts forward the view that spasmodic asthma is nothing more than a symptom of underlying nervous disorder. On what then is such a revolutionary claim based? Let us examine the clinical evidence.

The Man Who Escaped Death

Consider, for instance, the case of Mr. ——. 'Doctor,' he said, 'since I had a talk to you three weeks ago, I have had no asthma!' Three weeks before he had come for a consultation and gave a history of having suffered from asthma for over seventeen years. Now, a 'miracle worker' or 'faith healer' may have been satisfied to 'call it a day,' for there is much that is dramatic and satisfying in the achievement of such a quick 'cure.' The interests of medicine, however, demand a scientific explanation for this apparent 'miracle.' What then had happened?

The patient, over sixty years of age, had stated at the first consultation that his original attack occurred at about the age of forty-five when he woke up one night 'choking for breath.' The doctor who was called by his alarmed relatives stated that he had 'asthma,' and the patient had gone on having asthmatic attacks periodically every day and night since then.

He could not remember anything which might have caused it. However, it was explained to the patient that hypnosis would be able to help by teaching him to relax. All that his drugs and inhalations could do was to relax the muscular spasms of the bronchioles which caused his asthma, and it was pointed out that if he could learn to relax them naturally there would be no more asthma. He was given a simplified explanation of his condition. Fear and anxiety, he was told, caused nervous tension and made the patient hold himself tight and tense—literally tensed and ready to 'fight or run away.'

Holding the chest and lungs 'tight' resulted in asthma, and fear of this caused more tension than ever, which in turn brought on more asthmatic attacks and so created a vicious circle. Now, it was stated, he was afraid of his asthma and it was only the fear which kept it going. If he could learn to give up being afraid and cease holding himself tensed and ready to fight it then the asthma would go away. Nevertheless something had first started him being afraid, and although he could not remember any such incident now, he was told that he would be able to do so during the course of hypnotic treatment and that he would see that he did not have to be afraid any more.

The patient left with the promise to return later for a short course of treatment. As we have seen, when he did return in three weeks' time he was apparently cured. What had happened? First of all, the patient was highly suggestible, and although no attempt was made to hypnotise him in the ordinary sense of the word, he had, nevertheless, been greatly impressed by the simple, positive, direct explanation of his hitherto mysterious and dreaded complaint to such an extent that it had amounted to almost hypnotic suggestion. He had accepted the idea that he had no real disease at all and that his 'asthma' was only due to nervous tension resulting from fear and that if he gave up being afraid it would be unable to attack him. The hope raised, and the feeling of relief which followed, had indeed dispelled much of his nervous tension and the relaxation had brought about his apparent 'miracle cure.'

During the course of treatment, which consisted of four sessions of light hypnosis and suggestion, he was informed that the memory of what had first frightened him and caused difficulty in breathing would come into his mind some time on its own account. As a result he would see where his 'asthma' had come from, and so would understand that things were different now and that he did not have to be afraid any more.

A week or so later the patient reported that a 'thought had flashed into his mind'—something he had not thought of for many, many years. Apparently, just before the onset of his 'asthma' several years ago, he had been involved in a traffic accident from which he had been lucky to escape death. He had seen the danger approaching but had felt 'paralysed with fear.' A few nights after the incident and seemingly after he had recovered from the shock, to all outward appearances, he had awakened in the night sweating with fear and 'choking for breath.'

This then was the origin of his asthma, and the mechanism was no doubt as follows. First of all the accident gave rise to fear and anxiety. This by acting on the autonomic nervous system gave rise to tension. The tension expressed itself mainly in the lungs (by coincidence the patient happened to have a bronchial cold at the time so that attention was drawn to the lungs), and difficulty in breathing resulted in 'asthma.' Fear of 'asthma' created more nervous tension, which in turn cause more asthmatic attacks and so created a vicious circle.

(See Diagram 3.) The patient's whole attention being concentrated on his alarming and distressing condition, it is small wonder he forgot the precipitating incident. When he could relax as the result of hypnosis he ceased to occupy all his mind with the vicious circle and so could remember the incident easily. Full understanding of the cause removed the fear of the unknown, and so consolidated the cure.

This case illustrates several points of considerable importance.

That an incident (or idea) of sufficient emotional importance can by acting on the nervous system give rise to serious symptoms such as 'asthma.' These may occur at any age and not necessarily in early childhood as the Freudians believe.

That 'asthma' is not a disease *but only a symptom* of underlying nervous disorder.

That the usual, ordinary medical measures in a case such as this are only symptomatic and completely unscientific—a criticism incidentally which is often levelled quite unjustly at hypnotism! It is not much good giving injections and inhalants to relax the musculature of the bronchioles when all the time the thought which is causing the spasms lies festering in the mind.

That a cure can be brought about even in a severe case of seventeen years' standing by means of light hypnosis and suggestion.

That the cure to be complete does *not* consist of merely inducing a trance and saying 'Now you are well.' Undoubtedly an apparent 'cure' was brought about by the first consultation, but unless this had been consolidated it would have quite likely been of only temporary duration.

That forgotten memories of events which have caused trouble can be brought back to mind very simply and easily without years of psychoanalytical treatment or any so-called 'deep' hypnosis.

In most cases at least four or six sessions of hypnotic suggestion at weekly intervals are required to bring about a cure, but the same underlying principles can be detected in all of them. The following cases are typical of many in which the condition diagnosed as 'asthma' has proved to be no real disease at all but merely a symptom of underlying nervous anxiety, and readily amenable to treatment by hypnotic suggestion. This has been directed towards finding the cause of the anxiety and then removing it by appropriate suggestions, re-educating the patient in the process so that he is able to face up to and overcome conditions which previously upset him. Treatment does *not* consist of merely attempting to suppress the symptom of asthma by direct suggestion. It is submitted that hypnotic suggestion properly used is far more scientific than the usual 'orthodox' method of merely treating symptoms only by means of injections and sprays.

The Girl Who Was Let Down

Miss ——, a young single woman of twenty-five, reported with a history of severe attacks of spasmodic 'asthma' for over eight years. Her doctor wrote that she had had all the usual investigations and was apparently sensitive to various things such as house dust, etc., but that treatment had had no real effect.

She still called him out at night to give her injections and she carried an inhaler with her on all occasions.

The patient stated that she got an attack 'whenever she thought of it,' and if by chance she forgot her inhaler or forgot to fill it up she would have an attack immediately she noticed it. From her story it appeared that she had fallen in love with her first real 'boy friend' at about the age of seventeen. Everything had gone smoothly for a short time, but evidently the young man had had a roving eye and she became more and more jealous. This led to rows and arguments, during and after which she felt 'worked up' and 'unable to get her breath properly.' Finally he became tired of her accusations and went off with another girl. The patient stated that she felt 'heart broken' and 'wanted to die.'

Shortly after this, she began to have attacks of breathlessness which the local doctor diagnosed as 'asthma.' This terrified her, because she had seen a relative suffer from this complaint. The fear caused nervous tension, which in turn created more 'asthma,' and the patient was soon in the grip of a vicious circle. Six sessions of light hypnosis and suggestion at weekly intervals were sufficient to teach her to relax completely, realise that she had no real disease to fear at all, and re-educate her mind so that it could adopt an adult attitude to an adolescent affair. As a result, at the end of the course, she was able to report herself completely free of the dread disease 'asthma.' Words and ideas had done what medicine could not.

The Man Who Was 'Browned Off'

This young single man of about thirty-two reported with a history of frequent and severe 'asthma' attacks over several years.

Apparently after active service in the war he had been sent abroad to the tropics and kept there although the war was over. He began to get more and more irritated and 'fed up' with the heat and boredom. Shortly after he became 'properly browned off,' as he put it, he began to wake up at night 'struggling for breath.' This rapidly became worse and he was soon invalided out of the Service with 'asthma.'

By now he was afraid of his 'asthma,' and far from getting better on leaving the Service, as he had expected, he became steadily worse. Again the same principles of treatment were applied. The patient received an explanation of how his trouble had started and an assurance that if he followed instructions and learned to relax naturally he would have no more asthma to fear. Six sessions at weekly intervals were sufficient to readjust his attitude to life in general and dispel all his 'asthma.'

The Woman Who Was Afraid of Sickness

Mrs. ——, a happily married woman of about forty-five, reported with a history of severe 'asthma' attacks since the age of twenty or so. Apparently she had had a lot of worry and anxiety, as her parents had both died of distressing illnesses when she was about twenty. This left her to bring up the rest of the family. She had a great fear of becoming ill and unable to look after them properly. Soon she noticed herself getting attacks of breathlessness. These worried her excessively and soon developed into typical attacks of spasmodic 'asthma.' For years she tried all sorts of injections, drugs and inhalants without any real relief. Yet after several sessions of hypnosis she developed sufficient confidence to undertake a long trip abroad, and later, on her return, was able to report that she had been free from her once dreaded 'asthma.'

The Man Who Had an Operation

This middle-aged man reported with a history of severe asthmatic attacks over many years. The attacks were particularly severe on first waking up. An examination of his history revealed the fact that he had first experienced trouble with breathing after an operation. First of all he had hated the 'choking sensation of having the "mask" ' put over his face. Then, apparently, he had had the bad luck to develop a chest complaint after the anaesthetic, as does sometimes occur. He had, indeed, awakened from the anaesthetic with an irritating cough which soon led on to some degree of breathlessness.

Unfortunately the operation had not been a success, and in all he had to have three operations. He dreaded each one, and on each occasion he awakened from the anaesthetic with a cough and 'breathlessness.' Soon after leaving hospital he began to awaken in the night with attacks of breathlessness which the doctor diagnosed as 'asthma.' He became frightened of these, and, indeed, feared to go to sleep at night. The condition was not improved by the fact that he had seen his father 'suffer terribly with asthma' and finally die of it.

Because he at first confused hypnosis with sleep (of which he was afraid) he proved to be a difficult subject, but after half a dozen sessions he was able to report a disappearance of his fears and freedom from 'asthma.'

These, and hundreds of similar cases, show that there is a very real place for medical hypnotic suggestion as a means of manipulating the patient's imagination scientifically in order to free him of a complaint which has been brought about more often than not accidentally by the wrong use of that same imagination. Asthma is not a disease at all but merely a symptom—a symptom of an underlying nervous irritation—and the patient is far more likely to be sensitive to an irritating mother-in-law, an unfaithful spouse, a broken love affair or an impending bankruptcy than the usual substances such as feathers, house dust or various pollens which are invariably blamed by the orthodox believers in allergy. Even these will admit a fact, which has been often proved, that an asthmatic alleged to be sensitive or 'allergic' to, say, a rose, will have an attack if shown an artificial rose, providing he thinks it is real. To what else then can asthma be due except suggestion?

Chapter Ten

WAKING HYPNOSIS AND INSOMNIA

EVERY NIGHT OVER a million people in Britain fight hard to keep awake. They comprise the vast army of martyrs to insomnia which consumes 15 per cent of all National Health prescriptions in the form of sedatives. Records of cases show that fear of sleep is the real cause of insomnia. By the time the patient seeks treatment he is afraid that lack of sleep will cause ill health, and it is this very fear of insomnia which keeps it going. Nature has arranged that in time of fear or danger a man gets ready 'to fight or run away.'

Tension is the natural result. It is this tension, and not the lack of sleep, which causes the patient to feel more exhausted in the morning than when he went to bed. Even when forced into sleep by heavy doses of sedatives the patient's muscles remain on guard so that he feels 'half dead' in the morning.

It is just as though the patient were invited to sleep in a lion's den, and told 'Don't worry about the animal—take a nice big capsule and go to sleep.' Every instinct would shriek 'Danger' and the patient would strain every fibre of his being to stay awake to protect himself.

However, investigation shows that in every case of insomnia there is always a hidden deeper fear which makes sleep appear dangerous or anxiety-provoking to the patient. More often than not this is a very simple and ordinary thing.

Experience has proved that 'double-bed dilemmas,' 'twin-bed troubles' and 'marital muddles' are often the fundamental causes of insomnia. The following cases are typical.

Mr. ——, a middle-aged married man, complained of severe insomnia for several years. Hypnotherapy revealed a very simple cause which he had forgotten. Shortly before his insomnia had started he had been at a party where everybody had been vastly amused by some gossip about a man who talked in his sleep. Having a guilty conscience Mr. —— sub-consciously feared he might reveal his indiscretions to his wife. As a result he subconsciously fought against sleep, while he consciously took sleeping tablets to bring it on! Explanation and reassurance under hypnosis that he could sleep peacefully without fear of revealing his indiscretions soon dispelled his insomnia.

Mrs. ——, a middle-aged married woman, reported that she had 'hardly slept a wink' for years. Under the influence of hypnosis she was able to recall when it started. Apparently her husband snored and they decided to sleep in separate rooms. Subconsciously she began to worry and regard bedtime and sleep as symbolic of losing her husband. Hypnotherapy enabled her to readjust her ideas to such an extent that she could once more sleep with her husband. 'You know,' she said, 'his snores send me to sleep and they make me feel so safe!'

Mr. ——, a middle-aged business man, complained that he could sleep only in a chair. Once in bed he would be wide awake. Hypnosis revealed the hidden association between bed, sleep and danger in his mind. Badly injured in the war he had spent a long time in hospital undergoing many painful operations. Naturally the mere thought of bed and sleep jerked him wide awake. A few sessions of hypnosis enabled him to dispel this harmful association so that he looked forward to bed and sleep with pleasurable anticipation instead of fear.

Mr. and Mrs. ——, a young married couple, were the victims of 'twin-bed trouble.' They decided to change back to twin beds because their 'smart set' thought double beds 'too dread-fully old-fashioned.' Soon both began to suffer from insomnia, and hypnosis quickly revealed why. Secretly each had begun to wonder *why* twin beds had been suggested. Mr. —— worried whether Mrs. —— really loved him enough, and she did the same. Soon both were consuming large doses of sleeping drugs. Hypnotherapy enabled them to resolve their groundless fears and give up regarding sleep and bedtime as symbolic of separation, so that their insomnia soon disappeared.

Mr. ——, a middle-aged widower, was the victim of a 'night-shirt nightmare.' He had suffered from insomnia for many years. Apparently his wife had been rather a health crank, and suddenly took it into her head that he should wear a nightshirt!

Mr. —— used to sweat at the idea of his neighbours seeing the flapping horror on the wash-line. He sweated even more at the idea of opposing his wife. For years he looked forward to bed-time and sleep with dread. Insomnia soon resulted, and worry over this kept it going long after his wife had died. Hypnosis enabled Mr. —— to realise there was no longer any need to fear, with the result that he soon slept naturally.

These and countless other similar cases show that there is practically always a very simple cause of insomnia. This is seldom apparent to the victim, because he is so occupied with his fight against insomnia that he has forgotten the original trouble.

Hypnotherapy, by relaxing the mind, breaks the vicious circle, enables the patient to realise the cause of his trouble, see things in their proper perspective, and face up to his problems in a normal manner.

Sleeping pills are more likely to cause insomnia than cure it, because the patient soon finds he has to take ever-increasing doses and then worries about 'taking drugs.'

Modern hypnotherapy, by getting quickly to the root of the trouble and treating the cause, is a much more logical and scientific approach than merely suppressing symptoms with drugs. Modern 'waking hypnosis' bears no relation to the old-fashioned 'go-to-sleep variety.' With modern methods the patient literally 'wakes up to himself' to go to sleep!

Chapter Eleven

HYPNOSIS AND ALCOHOLISM

BY REASON OF its widespread social as well as individual consequences alcoholism has always presented a serious problem. The amiable drunkard so often portrayed in book, stage or screen stories is no object of amusement to his relatives in real life. Countless lives have been ruined, marriages broken up, careers spoilt and untold misery brought about by addiction to alcohol. The essential nature of the problem has remained obscure, and alcoholism has been regarded variously as being simply a disease in itself, either biochemical or allergic in nature, or merely the symptom of an underlying nervous disorder.

As may be expected when the exact nature of the condition is uncertain, the treatments advocated have been both numerous and varied. These range from medical procedures, using drugs such as apomorphine, emetin and the recently discovered Antabuse, which make it impossible to take alcohol without unpleasant effects, to moral and religious influences exerted by the Church, temperance societies, and groups such as Alcoholics Anonymous.

Medical treatment usually means treatment in an institution in order to make sure that the patient carries out the treatment and has no access to alcohol. In addition some treatments are not without danger, and cases of death have been reported during Antabuse therapy even in apparently healthy individuals.

Group therapy such as that employed by Alcoholics Anonymous means attendance at meetings of fellow sufferers where the alcoholic is urged and persuaded to refrain from drinking, no matter how much he may desire to do so.

Institutional and the latter treatment also, to a lesser extent, carries a certain amount of stigma, and the alcoholic is apt to regard himself as someone who is definitely outside the run of ordinary human beings. This suggestion, for reasons which we will see later, is not at all desirable.

All these treatments, mental, moral, religious or medical, have at least one thing in common—they can all claim a percentage of successes. It is by no means unknown for an alcoholic to 'see the light' at a religious meeting and to give up drinking completely, while medical and psychotherapeutic measures have their quota of successes.

This fact, that all common methods of treating alcoholism have a percentage of successes, throws an interesting light on the possible nature of its cause.

What relationship can there be between religious and medical methods of treatment? What becomes of the theory of bio-chemical and allergic origins of alcoholism when psycho-therapeutic measures effect a cure? What in fact does happen to the confirmed drunkard who suddenly gives up alcohol for good? It is undeniable that cases of almost instantaneous cure do occur. In such cases the general conditions affecting the patient remain the same. His personal history, often of nervous-ness, anxiety and hardship, remains the same. Factors alleged to have influenced his downfall, social conditions, family troubles or financial worries remain the same. Only one thing has changed—the patient's mind—and he thinks (and feels) 'I have no desire for alcohol,' whereas before he thought, 'I must have alcohol.' What can bring about such a radical change of mind, often in the space of only a few minutes? Under what conditions do we find similar extraordinary changes?

Those familiar with hypnosis will be fully aware of the extraordinary mental changes which can be brought about in this condition. It is unfortunately a common experience to see completely sober people behaving like drunkards at the command of some stage or amateur hypnotist. Although such spectacles are completely unedifying and undesirable, they serve to show the amazing changes which can be produced in a suggestible person. Stage hypnotists work only with highly suggestible subjects whom they deliberately select from volunteers by means of simple tests. Such people can be very deeply influenced and will often carry out the most compli-cated post-hypnotic suggestions.

Naturally, no responsible person would suggest such a thing, but it is highly likely that a deeply hypnotised person who could be persuaded to act like a drunkard would respond to a post-hypnotic suggestisn to the effect that he would desire alcohol. This would be all the more likely if he could be cleverly persuaded that 'alcohol was good for him'—that he 'needed alcohol to keep his strength up,' etc.

We know that self-hypnosis is an established fact and that in people who can achieve this state the most remarkable effects such as anaesthesia can be obtained. Is it possible that alcoholism can be due to accidental self-hypnosis? How could this come about? When we examine the history of an alcoholic we can usually divide it into three stages.

First of all, alcohol is taken for social reasons and the patient has the idea firmly fixed in his head that it is 'the thing to do,' that drinking makes him 'one of the crowd,' that drinking is 'manly' or 'sophisticated' and that people who do not drink are 'queer' or 'out of it.'

Secondly, there is nearly always a period of stress or strain when alcohol is taken in increasing amounts. During this period alcohol is regarded as a friend, for it smooths over the difficulties and apparently makes life easier.

Finally, in every alcoholic there comes a time when he suddenly realises that he cannot face things without drink. This is a time of emotional panic and the patient has fearful visions of going downhill to ruin 'like Uncle Henry,' or his father, 'who drank himself to death,' or some acquaintance who 'finished up in an asylum.'

We know that emotion sensitises the brain to hypnosis and that when emotion enters the picture reason is relegated to the background. An idea introduced in this condition has all the force of a strong hypnotic suggestion. Can we regard alcoholism as the result of a post-hypnotic suggestion self-given in an accidentally self-induced hypnotic state?

Certainly the behaviour of the alcoholic would seem to support the theory. Few alcoholics like alcohol, but feel compelled to take it against their better judgment, in much the same way as a deeply hypnotised person will later, in the waking state, feel compelled to carry out some foolish post-hypnotic suggestion.

Another point in favour is that alcoholics are usually very suggestible and make good hypnotic subjects, so that the possibility of their having hypnotised themselves is very likely.

It should be noted that contrary to popular belief it is not necessary to 'fall asleep,' 'close the eyes' or be 'stretched out and sat upon,' as in stage shows, to be hypnotised. Even in such shows during exhibitions of 'mass hypnosis,' dozens of people in the audience in full waking state will be found who are unable to 'unlock' their clasped hands until permitted to do so by the hypnotist.

Finally there is the undisputed fact that hypnosis when properly used can and does cure cases of long-standing alcoholism. It is a fundamental law that what can be caused by suggestion can be cured by suggestion, and even in all the orthodox treatments there is a big element of suggestion. In treating alcoholism by hypnosis it is not sufficient or desirable to employ the usual naïve stage or amateur technique by simply saying, 'Now you cannot drink,' 'Drink will make you sick,' etc. Treatment should be aimed at enabling the patient not only to give up alcohol but teaching him how to face life and its problems in an adult fashion so that there can be no relapse. With proper planning this can be done in a relatively short space of time and using only a light to medium form of hypnosis which practically anybody can achieve. Usually a preliminary session to discuss the case and explain the nature of the treatment, followed by half a dozen sessions of hypnosis, is sufficient to establish a cure.

Treatment by hypnosis has the advantage that there is no stigma attached to it as with institutional treatment, and patients can continue at their occupations and live an ordinary life. One condition is essential—the patient must really want to get well. The man who applies for treatment because he fears going down to ruin and desperately wants to give up drinking can be easily cured. The man who is dragged along by his wife to be cured, and who secretly has no desire to be cured, is unlikely to respond very easily, if at all. Fortunately such cases are few and far between and the majority of victims are only too anxious to co-operate.

The following cases will give some idea of the value of hypnosis in the treatment of alcoholism.

Professional Man, 45

The patient had been in the habit of taking excessive alcohol over a period of years. He had started drinking in the usual way, first of all on social occasions, then increasing gradually to ease the strain of professional work, until he realised suddenly that he could not face life without it. If unable to get ordinary alcoholic drinks he would even drink methylated spirits. Various treatments had been tried without success and the patient was rapidly going downhill. Five sessions of hypnosis at weekly intervals were sufficient to remove the craving entirely. There has been no relapse over a considerable period of time and his wife reports that he is mentally, morally and physically a different man. His doctor wrote: 'I am very interested in —— because he was cured by hypnotism while actually drinking and when institutional and other treatment had entirely failed.'

Mrs. ——, 50

This patient had had a very hard and tragic life. She had started drinking socially but increased the dose and frequency to ease the shock of losing her first husband. When her second husband was killed and she lost her only daughter in tragic circumstances she took more and more alcohol to drown her sorrow. Eventually she realised with a shock that she could not do without it and had fearful visions of what her end would be, as 'there was drink in the family.' When seen she was drinking a bottle of whisky a day and all other treatment had failed. A few sessions of hypnosis were sufficient to establish a complete cure and there has been no relapse over a long period in spite of trying conditions.

Married Man, 40

The patient had started drinking during service abroad, merely as a social habit. This increased to ease general worries and responsibilities in later life. Realisation that he relied on alcohol so much came as a great shock to him, as he had 'seen what it had done to others.' When seen, the patient was drinking heavily and trying to forget. A few sessions removed all desire for drink, and over a year later his doctor wrote to say: '. . . he has been quite free of any tendency to alcoholism since he had hypnotic treatment.'

Mrs. ——, 50

This patient had been introduced to alcohol in her schooldays abroad, where, apparently, on special feast days the whole school received enough to make them merry! She continued drinking socially, but increased the dose considerably when she lost her husband. After a time the patient suddenly realised with a shock how much she depended upon alcohol. She became afraid of her future as 'there was drink in the family.' When seen she was drinking very heavily—was never really sober in fact—and even took bottles of drink to bed with her. Again a few sessions of hypnotic suggestion were sufficient to abolish the craving completely.

Mrs. ——, 45

This patient began drinking for social reasons. As her social duties increased, involving personal appearances under rather trying conditions, she drank more and more to cover up her nervousness. She realised suddenly with a shock how much she relied upon alcohol and had visions of 'finishing up in an asylum like her father.' From then on she drank more and more, endeavouring to drown this and other fears. All orthodox treatment had been unable to help, but she responded perfectly to a few sessions of hypnosis.

Mr. ——, Married Man, 45

This case is especially interesting because it is generally believed that an alcoholic cannot drink sociably but must give up alcohol of all kinds completely if he wants to be cured. This patient had started drinking to be 'one of the crowd,' but increased the dose to enable him to face business worries. There was a history of alcoholism in the family and the patient suddenly conceived a great fear of going downhill. This caused him to drink more than ever. The patient insisted, against advice, that he must be allowed to drink beer in moderation 'for business reasons,' but begged to be freed from the curse of alcohol in the form of spirits, to which he was addicted. He was warned that it was generally considered impossible for an alcoholic to do this. However, as he insisted, he was treated with hypnosis and reported himself free from any desire for spirits. A year later his wife wrote to say: '. . . he has been quite all right since having hypnotic treatment and is wonderfully changed. He is now able to manage a new business. He still drinks beer, but that is all, and that is in fact a stern test indeed. I know this to be true because I could always tell immediately when he had been drinking spirits or wines and now I am confident of his cure.'

Although not generally advised, this case and others like it show that it is possible for a former alcoholic to drink sociably. Hypnotism is not a 'cure all' and will almost certainly fail in cases which have no real desire to be cured. A typical case was that of Mr. ——, who was forced to apply for treatment (very reluctantly) by his wife. As she had told him she would leave him if he did not stop drinking, and as this was the one thing he desired, then it was not surprising that co-operation was nil and hypnosis failed!

These typically successful cases, however, and many others like them show that there is a very real place for hypnosis in the treatment of alcoholism.

Chapter Twelve

HYPNOSIS AND THE BRAIN BARRIER

HYPNOSIS CAN BREAK through the 'brain barrier.' This barrier is the most constant feature to be found in those suffering from psychological disorders; the following facts show that it is a very real barrier.

It prevents the patient doing what he really wants. This explains why a patient will say: 'My reason tells me that I should do so and so. I want to do it, but I can't.'

It prevents the doctor, or the well-meaning friend, from helping the patient with ordinary advice. Exhortations, such as the usual 'Come on, pull yourself together,' have no effect. They simply do not get through the brain barrier. Many an unjustly labelled 'Weary Willie' could be more fairly described as 'Brain Barrier Bill'!

One of the most classical cases in history is that of the great musician Sergei Rachmaninoff. When the composer's First Symphony was played at St. Petersburg in 1897, it was a dismal failure. The next day criticisms such as this appeared:

'If there were a conservatoire in Hell, Rachmaninoff would get first prize for his symphony, so devilish are the discords he places before us.'

Rachmaninoff became worried and depressed. When he tried to write a new concerto, he was unable to do so. Even the great Tolstoy, whom Rachmaninoff deeply admired, was unable to help him with ordinary advice.

However, Dr. Dahl, practising in Moscow, was able to break through the brain barrier by hypnotism. Rachmaninoff had daily treatment from January to April 1900, and before the end of the year two movements of the concerto had been completed. Rachmaninoff scored a great success as a soloist at a concert in Moscow where this work was played.

The Nature of the Brain Barrier

Modern research in hypnotherapy has revealed the nature of this brain barrier. It can be artificially created under controlled conditions in the laboratory. For instance, if a good hypnotic subject is told, 'You cannot pronounce your own name,' he will be unable to do so. An artificial 'brain barrier' has been created. Under experimental, controlled conditions it can, of course, be as easily removed.

What is the mechanism behind this phenomenon? We know that hypnosis is really only a superconcentration of the mind. (See Diagram 1.) Normally the mind is occupied with a thousand and one different thoughts. Ordinary suggestion and advice literally 'goes in one ear and out of the other,' so that only a few scattered parts of the mind take notice, and the effect is correspondingly weak.

In hypnosis, where the mind is superconcentrated, practically all the mind—or the major part of it, at least—takes in the suggestion, so that the effect is strong.

Emotion, we know, concentrates the mind. Superconcentration of the mind is hypnosis. Therefore any sufficiently strong emotion can concentrate the mind into a condition of hypnosis. Any idea which enters the mind at this time will have the force of a hypnotic suggestion.

Careful examination of a patient suffering from psychoneurotic or psychosomatic disorder will always reveal at least one strongly emotional incident. Contrary to Freud's idea, this may occur at any age, not necessarily in childhood.

Such a patient has literally hypnotised himself—accidentally, it is true, in most cases. He has accidentally created his own brain barrier and in fact is *en rapport* with himself. With his brain concentrated on his own ideas, he is unable to concentrate upon the ideas of others.

Typical symptoms of the brain barrier are:

Difficulty in Concentration

This is due to the fact that, with most of his mind concentrated upon his troubles, there is little, if any, mind left to concentrate on other things.

Loss of Interest

As the patient has his attention concentrated on his own woes and troubles, he takes little interest in anything else.

Poor Memory

As the patient is unable to concentrate on things, and takes little interest in them, it is not surprising that he is unable to remember them.

Psychosomatic Symptoms

Fear concerning his condition gives rise to nervous tension. This may give rise to all sorts of conditions such as insomnia, migraine, asthma and 'panic attacks.' Worry over these merely increases the nervous tension and creates a vicious circle.

The patient with a psychological disorder presents much the same problem as a subject who has been hypnotised by somebody else. It is necessary to induce hypnosis and establish *rapport* before attempting to deal with conditions resulting from suggestions by the previous hypnotist—the patient himself, in the naturally occurring case.

Difficulty is to be expected in both cases. This explains why nervous patients seldom make good hypnotic subjects at the first attempt. Being *en rapport* with themselves, they resist, and training is required to establish a new *rapport* with the hypnotist.

The patient is taught to relax, see things clearly and realise the simple cause of the condition. His mind is then re-educated and strengthened, so that he can deal with his problems in an adult manner.

Now let us look at some typical cases.

Insomnia

Mr. ——, an accountant, started reciting figures in his sleep. His jealous wife decided that the magic figures 36-23-36 had more to do with so-called 'vital statistics' of some film star than with his work. Rows and arguments followed. Mr. —— remembered that he had talked in his sleep as a boy. Fear that he might disclose some past escapades in his sleep caused him to become emotionally worked up. The idea crept in that it was positively dangerous for him to go to sleep! Worry over the resulting insomnia merely created a vicious circle, and kept the condition going long after the original cause had been forgotten. Failing memory, poor concentration, and loss of interest in his work caused further worry and aggravated his condition.

Hypnotherapy was able to break through his 'brain barrier' and let him see things in their true proportions. He was able to accept the idea that he could sleep without talking. This removed all imagined 'danger' from sleep, and so his insomnia rapidly disappeared.

Asthma

Mrs. ——, a young married woman, complained of severe attacks of asthma. Investigation revealed that she was really worried because she had married her cousin. Foolish friends had frightened her with stories that any child she had might be mentally defective. Just before her baby had been born, she became so emotionally worked up that she 'couldn't get her breath.'

This choking feeling frightened her, and the idea of asthma was implanted in her head. Fear of this created a vicious circle, and recurrent attacks were soon common. As her mind became more and more occupied with her asthma, Mrs. —— took less and less interest in anything else. Hypnotherapy was able to break through the barrier, remove her fears and reassure her, with the result that she was soon free of asthma attacks.

Migraine

Mr. ——, an ambitious young clerk, studied hard to improve himself. Nervous tension and overwork caused a few headaches. Unfortunately he caught a heavy cold and developed sinusitis, with pains in the head. Prevented from taking his examinations by this illness, he became emotionally worked up. The idea developed that there was something seriously wrong with his head. Worry over this caused such tension that he began to have severe migraine attacks. Preoccupation with his fears and symptoms caused him to lose interest in his work. This, with loss of concentration and failing memory, convinced him that he must have 'something like a brain tumour.' By hypnotherapy it was possible to break through this brain barrier and convince him that there was nothing seriously wrong with his head. Reassured that he could make a success of life in spite of the temporary setback, he soon ceased to have any migraine.

'Panic Attacks'

Miss ——, an attractive young woman, complained of attacks of 'panic.' These occurred for apparently no reason. They prevented her going to work or leading any kind of social life. Investigation revealed that they started when she first went to work. Developing a 'crush' on her elderly married employer, who knew nothing of it, she felt 'guilty.' She feared that others in the office would guess her secret. As a result, she began to get attacks of 'panic' on going to work. These frightened her so much that soon she had to give up her position. By the time she came for treatment, she expected 'panic attacks,' so that they occurred on practically any occasion, although the original cause had long been forgotten. Hypnotherapy was able to break through her vicious circle of thinking and, this barrier removed, it proved easy to restore her confidence.

. . . . .

Points which may help doctors to prevent patients developing a full-scale brain barrier are:

Examine carefully all ideas which developed in the patient's mind during a strongly emotional period.

Find and treat the root cause of the trouble when faced with psychosomatic symptoms. Asthma, migraine, insomnia and a host of other conditions usually have an emotional basis.

Get the patient to relax so that he can think clearly, and concentrate on the doctor's advice. Remember the usual exhortations are not absorbed when the patient is tense and anxious.

Appeal to the patient's imagination instead of will-power to help him. Insomnia, for instance, is more likely to be overcome if the patient pictures (or imagines) himself going to sleep. Using will-power, gritting the teeth, and saying 'I will sleep' will merely keep him wide awake.

If these simple 'first aid' measures fail, the doctor should consider trying hypnotherapy first, instead of as a last resort. Hypnotism is the only simple psychotherapeutic procedure which can produce, demonstrate and remove the brain barrier under experimental conditions. It is therefore logically the first choice of treatment to get through and remove naturally occurring cases of brain-barrier trouble.

Chapter Thirteen

HYPNOSIS AND BALDNESS

Do MEN SHED hair instead of tears? Is baldness a stress disease, like duodenal ulcer, or high blood pressure? Casual observation in any theatre reveals the shining domes of tired business men, alternating with the elaborate coiffures of their consorts. This confirms practically the only real fact about baldness known to medical science—men get it more than women. The great question is—why?

As usual in medicine, when practically nothing is known concerning the real cause of any condition, there are innumerable theories to explain it. Glandular disorders, hereditary factors, even vitamin deficiencies or excess all have their advocates. Most of them could equally well apply to women. They do not explain why baldness should be almost exclusively a male prerogative, and why it should affect certain men and not others.

The baldness we are dealing with here is that which results from diffuse hair-fall for no apparent reason, which sooner or later leaves the scalp naked, but often not unashamed. We are not concerned with the well-known loss of hair which may occur after certain fevers or severe illnesses, or that which may result from actual disease of the scalp.

'Tight feelings' in the head commonly accompany nervous disorders, and there is some evidence to suggest that nervous tension may play a big part in causing the hitherto unexplained preponderance of baldness in men. The actual mechanism of the process may be due to a diminution of the blood supply to the scalp, with loss of nourishment to the hair, or the tension may literally strangle the roots, much akin to the old idea of baldness resulting from tight hats. Points in favour of a nervous origin for baldness are:

Men tend to bottle up their emotions. Women are more

likely to let go and obtain relief in a flood of tears. By keeping a 'stiff upper lip,' the strong silent man may be reserving for himself a bald upper pate! It is well known that emotions can cause glandular changes. Getting ready for 'fight or flight' causes the adrenal gland to pour out adrenalin. Increased adrenal androgen is believed to play a big part in the loss of hair. Investigation will show that most bald men have undergone prolonged strain of one kind or another. Big business and baldness would seem to go together.

Men who can let themselves go, and express their feelings in various ways, such as musicians, actors and artists, are usually well endowed with flowing locks. The few 'toupee-toting troubadours' and 'thinning Thespians' who would seem to be the exceptions to this rule may often be found to be the victims of other factors.

Men use their brains more than women. No doubt increased brain activity drains blood from the scalp and starves the hair. Even the area of baldness tends to indicate the type of mental activity. The 'high-brow' type of baldness, with patches receding from the forehead, is well known. It is significant that the frontal lobes of the brain are concerned with the obscure, higher psychological processes. The business man generally goes bald on top first. The baldness spreads over the sides (corresponding to the motor and sensory areas of the brain) as his activity continues. Modern big business involves much complex thinking and forethought, so that even the frontal, 'high-brow' areas are soon involved. The real 'go-getter' type seldom takes long to go bald all over. The horrid thought arises that with more and more women taking up business careers, baldness may eventually become as common in women as in men, just as the incidence of duodenal ulcer in women has increased. Will women eventually sacrifice curls for careers?

Men expect baldness, whereas women do not. Men are more imaginative than women. 'Toupee terror,' by creating fear, worry and anxiety in the prospective victim, creates tension, and probably helps to bring about the very condition he fears. Few men think of joining the ranks of the hairless with equanimity!

The observations of Sabouraud, the great French skin specialist, would seem to support the theory that mental processes are involved in the production of baldness. He noted that baldness was rare in peasants, who did hard physical work in the open, whereas it was common in sedentary and city workers, who presumably suffered more from mental stress.

Also it is well known that a severe nervous shock can cause the hair to change colour or fall out altogether. Is it not reasonable to suppose that a less spectacular but more prolonged nervous strain may bring about baldness? The following cases illustrate the influence of the mind on the hair.

Mr. ——, a young clerk, twenty-four, complained of overwhelming feelings of panic and anxiety. Investigation revealed that he was a typical case of 'toupee terror.' Following a lecture while in the Service on the care of the hair, he had accidentally put on somebody else's cap. This he considered to be dirty, and he developed a fear of scalp infection. When he noticed a few hairs falling out, his worst fears seemed to be confirmed. Shortly after this, his hair 'began to come out in handfuls.' The hair-fall continued even after he had left the Service and in spite of all treatment. When seen, he was convinced that he would soon be bald. A few sessions of hypnotherapy were sufficient to banish his fears, with the result that his hair began to grow again and he lost his feelings of panic and anxiety.

Mr. ——, a young business man of thirty, reported with symptoms of anxiety, insomnia, headache and profuse hair-fall. He stated that he had lost confidence in himself, could not concentrate on his business, and saw himself more like 'Dan Druff' than 'Dan Dare,' to use his own words. Investigation revealed him to be a typical 'receding Romeo.' With a history of baldness in the family, he developed a great fear of this condition on noticing a few hairs coming out on his brush. Being engaged, he also had a great fear of losing his fiancée as well as his hair. The symptoms of anxiety, insomnia, headache and loss of concentration were the results of this fear. Reassurance under hypnosis soon banished his groundless fear, the symptoms vanished, so that he kept his hair, and his fiancée as well.

Mr. ——, a business man of forty sought treatment for 'anxiety neurosis.' He suffered from what he called a 'domestic dome.' For years his wife had nagged him. One of her jibes was that he would soon go bald, and that she would leave him if he did. Strangely enough, his hair began to fall out 'in handfuls.' This was not surprising, as there was nothing he wished for more than to be rid of her! He obtained a divorce for another reason, but his hair continued to fall because he worried now about ba ⌐ ꭇess instead of his previous tormentor. He wished to marry again, but was afraid that baldness would prejudice his chances. A few sessions of hypnotherapy enabled him to adjust his point of view, lose his fears and retain his hair.

It is not necessary for a man to become unduly emotional to keep his hair. Any well-adjusted man should be able to control himself without developing baldness. There are many people with good heads of hair who have made a success of life. For those who are unable to manage things themselves, hypnotism can help.

Hypnotism cannot, of course, 'grow hair on a wooden leg,' but there is every reason to believe that hypnotic suggestion can affect the growth of hair just as it can influence any organ or gland in the body. It is well known that the mere idea of food can make the mouth 'water.' If a thought can make the salivary gland work, surely there is no reason to doubt that appropriate suggestions can influence other organs and glands, even those controlling the growth of hair.

Points which medical men will find of use in advising patients who consult them about their loss of hair are:

Raising hope may raise hair. Avoid depressing remarks about baldness being inevitable or hereditary. The so-called 'hereditary factor' is probably largely only bad suggestion—the patient going bald because he expects it.

Relaxing is probably the best restorer. Relaxation will dispel tension and give the hair a chance. It will benefit the patient in other ways as well.

Thinking can improve the 'thatch.' Positive suggestions of hair growth will overcome the negative ideas of baldness and give the patient the best possible help.

Chapter Fourteen

HYPNOSIS AND BEAUTY

WOMEN CAN THINK their way to beauty, fantastic as the idea may appear at first! Medical men have long disproved the old adage that 'beauty is only skin deep.' Now the new science of hypnotherapy is showing that the organs and glands essential to beauty can be controlled by thought. Nowhere can this be better demonstrated than in the skin. Few people think of the outer covering we present to the world as an organ, but it is really the largest in the body. With its countless thousands of tiny cells, nerves, glands and blood vessels it mirrors not only our health but often our very thoughts!

Who has not noticed the embarrassment of a friend or acquaintance who blushed scarlet? And what is a blush but a rush of blood to the face as the result of a thought dilating the blood vessels?

Working on these principles, scientists and doctors have produced some amazing results. Ullman,* for instance, by using concentrated suggestion has succeeded in raising real blisters on a patient by describing an imaginary burn.

Now, Mrs. —— had never heard of Ullman, but she had heard about that 'flighty widow' at the office! When she thought her husband paid more attention to the lady than was strictly necessary at the firm's annual ball, Mrs. —— was furious. 'That woman seemed to get right under my skin, doctor,' she said. After a jealous row with her husband, the patient found huge patches of skin covered with an ugly, blotchy red rash. It went away, of course, but the next time she began to dress for a dance it reappeared, and stopped her going. Soon it began to appear on any social occasion. Mrs. —— became worried and avoided going out more and more. When seen she had hardly been out

* Ullman, M., 'Herpes Simplex and Second Degree Burn Induced under Hypnosis,' *American Journal of Psychiatry*, 1947, **103**, 828–30.

of the house for years, and wore a veil, with a high-necked dress to hide her skin.

'Surely it couldn't be due to that woman, doctor?' said Mrs. ——. 'I've given up being jealous of her years ago.'

She was right. Her condition was not due to 'that woman,' but to her own foolish emotion! Jealousy had started the irritation but worry over her condition had developed into a vicious circle of fear and tension which kept it going.

Mrs. —— was reacting to 'danger' in much the same way as a chameleon—that simple little animal which thinks it can elude its enemies by changing the colour of its skin!

Records of the British Society of Medical Hypnotists reveal many such cases as that of Mrs. ——. Often the tension interferes with other organs and glands, so that conditions as widely separated as asthma, migraine or insomnia may result. The cause can nearly always be traced to an emotional incident, and, needless to say, such conditions take a heavy toll of beauty.

How then can things be put right? When the patient's mind is in a turmoil, such as that of Mrs. ——, ordinary suggestion is useless, as it literally 'goes in one ear and out the other.' The patient is unable to concentrate the mind and absorb the idea sufficiently to affect the nervous system. Hypnosis, by concentrating the mind, overcomes this difficulty and allows suggestion to act powerfully.

In the case of Mrs. —— it was possible to teach her in a few sessions how to relax, look at things sensibly and stop worrying about her condition, with the result that her skin gradually returned to normal.

It is strange indeed to think that open pores may be the sign of a shut-in personality, and a blotchy skin the evidence of pent-up emotion! Perhaps nothing could have a more devastating effect upon beauty than insomnia. Tired, lack-lustre eyes, with their tell-tale rings, betray sleepless nights spent tossing and turning. By the time the victim comes for treatment it is merely the fear or worry about insomnia which keeps it going, for Nature has arranged that in time of danger and anxiety one does not sleep. In every case, however, there is always some emotional incident which started the insomnia by implanting the idea that it would be dangerous, difficult or impossible to sleep.

Miss ——, a young business woman, complained that she had not slept without drugs for over five years. 'Half dead' in the mornings, she felt so tired during the day that it was all she could do to keep her job. Her social life was about 'nil' as she 'did not feel up to going out.' Investigation revealed that the insomnia had started while nursing a sick mother, who called her frequently during the night. The mother actually died in her sleep, but Miss —— had a guilty feeling that she might have slept while her mother needed help. Worry and anxiety over this caused insomnia, and worry over the insomnia kept it going even after the doctor had explained that her mother had died peacefully in her sleep, and that she had nothing with which to reproach herself. In her ordinary state this explanation could not help, but when her mind was concentrated by hypnosis it was able to absorb this consoling thought, so that Miss —— soon lost all her fear and slept naturally.

Tension is another great enemy of beauty. One has only to look at the wrinkled, drawn and often positively haggard faces to be seen every day to realise its shattering effect. Tension is Nature's method of preparing for 'fight or flight,' and is a natural response to any threatened danger. In our complex modern life the 'danger' varies, but to the nervous system one danger is just the same as another. Tension will be created whether the 'danger' is fear of ill-health, going bankrupt or losing a lover!

Mrs. —— described herself as a 'bundle of nerves.' At thirty-five she was tense, nervous and anxious, with a furrowed brow that gave her the appearance of bearing the cares of the whole world on her shoulders. Now she was worried about her looks. 'I'm sure my husband is losing interest in me,' she said, 'and I can't blame him. I'm so bad-tempered and irritable these days it's a wonder he puts up with me.' A few inquiries revealed that Mrs. ——'s condition had started with 'mother-in-law trouble' soon after her marriage. Fear of open rows and bottled-up emotions resulted in tension and anxiety. When she noticed the physical results of these—a few lines here, a wrinkle there and a generally strained appearance—she began to fear losing her looks and her husband. Worry over this merely increased her tension—and the lines!—long after the original mother-in-law problem had been solved and forgotten. Hypnosis enabled Mrs. —— to relax her body completely and absorb the idea in concentrated form that she could give up worrying. With the vicious circle of tension, strain and anxiety broken, Mrs. —— soon looked and felt years younger.

Emotions are powerful because they concentrate the mind into a condition akin to hypnosis. People who squander their emotions by continually saying 'I hate this' or 'I'm afraid of that' are simply hypnotising themselves into ill health.

Points which medical men may advise patients who want to give themselves a 'mental face-lift' may be summarised as follows.

Avoid:

Nagging. Remember nagging means 'sagging.'
Emotional exhaustion. 'Jaded wives are faded wives.'
Worry over trifles. Remember worry means wrinkles.
Temper tantrums. Temper means tension—and 'lines.'
Jealousy. Remember 'green eyes' are a jinx on beauty.
Malicious gossip. Scandalous 'claptrap' may mean a 'rat-trap mouth.'

Do:

Practice relaxation to dispel tension, so giving organs and glands a chance to work naturally.
Cultivate the habit of thinking cheerful, happy and healthy thoughts, which can influence the nervous system.
Learn to use the imagination constructively. Imaginary 'success pictures' in which the patient 'sees' herself in *the way she would like to be* promote feelings which can help to bring about the desired result.

Chapter Fifteen

PERSONAL APPEARANCE, NEUROSIS AND HYPNOTHERAPY

EXPERIENCE HAS SHOWN that many cases of anxiety neurosis arise from worry over physical defects or abnormalities in personal appearance.

Very often these defects appear unimportant to onlookers, but to the victim they may be unduly magnified.

Much misery and unhappiness result where patients become unduly sensitive. They tend to withdraw into themselves, and deliberately avoid normal social contact with others. This introspective attitude serves only to concentrate their minds on their troubles, so that a vicious circle of thinking is established.

Undoubtedly most people see themselves as they really are, while others may be unduly optimistic. The patients with whom we are concerned invariably paint their self-portraits in the darkest colours.

It is the attitude of mind that counts. Many stage and screen stars, for instance, suffer from defects, such as outstanding ears or abnormally large feet, yet they have not allowed these factors to hinder their progress. On the other hand, it is quite common to meet patients whose lives have been made a misery by some trifling defect that probably few others have noticed.

Such people seldom seek treatment for the basic trouble. Usually the complaint is that they 'feel inferior or ill at ease with people.' There may be actual 'attacks of panic' at the idea of mixing in the social round. The physical symptoms and 'feelings' which accompany fear may dominate the whole picture.

Thus there may be trembling or sweating, blushing, stammering, palpitation of the heart or 'butterflies in the stomach.' Even when the patient does recognise the cause of his anxiety he often hesitates to express it for fear of ridicule, and the secret usually has to be dragged out of him.

Imagine such a patient going to his general practitioner and complaining that his nose was too large or that he was worried because his ears stuck out!

Such things can, however, worry patients into a neurosis. A measure of the seriousness with which some people take such defects in personal appearance is the readiness with which they will face even plastic surgery in the hope of overcoming their troubles.

A remarkable fact is that long-continued thinking of themselves as despised figures or objects of ridicule can actually bring about changes in appearance, mannerisms and personality. They appear to throw themselves into a part. We are all familiar with the way a clever impersonator can mimic his victims and appear to change his whole appearance and personality.

The question is why do these patients play their unhappy parts on the stage of life?

The answer is probably that they are the victims of accidental self-hypnosis. It is known that a hypnotised person can mimic or play a suggested part with exceptional realism. How, when, why and where have these patients been hypnotised? When we examine case-histories carefully, there will always be found an emotional incident or even a series of such incidents that may be deemed responsible. Emotion, we know, concentrates the mind into a condition akin to, if not identical with, hypnosis; for hypnosis may be regarded as a superconcentration of the mind. Any idea introduced at this time will act with the force of a hypnotic suggestion—and, if disturbing enough, will set up a chain of disordered, emotional thinking which can lead to real neurosis.

The following cases are typical of patients one meets in hypnotherapeutic practice.

Mr. ——, a young, single clerk of about twenty-five, was sent for treatment because he suffered from attacks of panic. He avoided all normal social contacts as much as possible, and was so worried about his unpleasant symptoms that he could not remember the cause of the trouble. Under the influence of hypnosis, however, he was able to recall the painful incident that had started the trouble.

Apparently, at the impressionable age of fourteen, the patient had been nicknamed 'Punch' by his school-fellows because of his large nose. The idea stuck, and from then on the patient became more and more convinced that all his acquaintances were laughing at him.

A short course of hypnotherapy convinced him that many famous people, including the Duke of Wellington, had had large noses. Nobody, he was told, would dream of laughing at him now. He could give up worrying about 'Punch.'

Some time later he wrote to say that he had joined a club and was living a perfectly normal social life, having lost all his old nervous feelings.

Now it is obvious that hypnosis could not have changed the patient's features or his past history, but it did, by altering the way he looked at things, change his future life for the better.

Miss ——, a young typist of about twenty-five, was sent for treatment because she believed herself to be a social misfit. She was tall, thin and flat-chested; she was round-shouldered and wore glasses. Of all these defects she was painfully aware. She admitted that she did not dance or go to parties. When asked why she did not try to mix more with other people, she said that she 'felt awful' in company and was sure that others were laughing at her.

The case-history revealed that she had been regarded as the 'ugly duckling' of the family. She had always been overshadowed by her pretty sister, now happily married while the patient still lived with her parents. They told her 'it was a pity she wasn't more like her sister' and that it was time she 'bucked up' and 'pulled herself together.' Such exhortations failed to undo the harm caused during the emotional crises of childhood and adolescence when the patient had had to take second place to her sister.

As a result of such ideas, the patient saw herself only as an 'ugly duckling.' Under the influence of hypnosis, however, counter-suggestions had a much more powerful effect. Many plain women, she was told, enjoyed a full and happy life. Even famous actresses suffered from physical defects.

Tallness was no disadvantage if she learned to hold herself well and walk properly. Mannequins had to be tall and slim, and artificial aids were readily available for flat chests. As for her eyes, she could learn to wear contact lenses for social occasions instead of ugly glasses. Any good beauty parlour would work wonders for her hair and teach her the art of make-up. Fashion magazines would give her an idea how to dress. She could join a social club, learn to dance and form a circle of friends.

As these suggestions began to take effect, the patient felt for the first time that life might be really worth living. Some time later she wrote to say that she had joined a tennis club, learned to dance and had acquired a boy friend.

Such cases show that there is scope for hypnotherapy in a wide range of cases quite outside the province of 'orthodox' medicine. It is to be hoped that as this fact becomes more widely recognised, suitable cases will be referred for hypno-therapy in the early stages before complex neuroses have developed.

Chapter Sixteen

HYPNOSIS, LOVE AND PSYCHOSOMATIC DISORDERS

Poets have long speculated about the nature of love. Recent work in hypnotherapy throws new light on the subject. There appears to be a remarkable similarity between the state of the mind in love and hypnosis.

Records of many cases of asthma, migraine, insomnia, anxiety neurosis and allied disorders reveal that they have originated in a disturbance of that emotional state called love.

'Laggardly lovers,' 'cautious Casanovas,' 'bashful beaux,' 'frustrated females,' 'blushing belles,' 'jealous Juliets' and 'reluctant Romeos' feature high up in the list of those suffering from psychosomatic disorders.

Some of the most obvious points of similarity between love and hypnosis are:

Rapport

The person in love appears indifferent to the attractions of others, just as the hypnotised subject pays attention only to the hypnotist.

Hypersuggestibility

In love a person is easily swayed by the opinions of the loved one in the same way that the hypnotist can influence his subject by suggestion.

Mental and Physical Changes

Love may change the whole outlook of a person, even politics, religion or the habits of a lifetime. It is well known that love can affect the breathing, cause blushing, palpitation and even loss of appetite. Hypnosis can cause similar changes.

Universal Susceptibility

Love, like hypnosis, may occur irrespective of colour, race, age, religion or sex. It may occur suddenly—'love at first sight'—like practically instantaneous hypnosis in a highly suggestible subject. On the other hand it may develop gradually, just as a poor subject can be trained by repeated sessions to achieve hypnosis.

Frangibility

The spell of both love and hypnosis can be broken by an emotional shock of sufficient intensity. Thus love can turn to hatred, just as the subject can break the *rapport* with the hypnotist if he objects to a suggestion.

All these effects and points of similarity can be explained only if there exists a common factor in love and hypnosis. Modern research has stripped the veil of mystery from hypnosis and revealed it to be essentially a superconcentration of the mind. In love there is the same intense concentration on the object of affection. The actual physical changes, such as blushing or palpitation, are brought about through the action of the nervous system.

It is obvious, therefore, that widespread changes in the organs and glands can be expected when the mind is disturbed by any upset of this powerful emotional state. In speaking of love we generally mean that mixture of strong affection and tender regard accompanied by physical desire which occurs between members of the opposite sex.

The points raised, however, can apply equally well to other forms of love, such as mother love, and can even explain love between members of the same sex.

The importance of the state of mind in causing mental and physical illness has been somewhat overlooked in the past— probably because many patients do not tell their family doctors the truth—often for fear of embarrassment.

As one patient naïvely explained when taxed with not telling his doctor the truth: 'Well, I've known him all my life, play bridge with him and I'd have felt such a fool telling him about my love life.' He explained that he did not mind telling the hypnotist, because 'with hypnotism it would come out anyway.'

Most of these cases are referred by the doctors as cases of

insomnia, migraine, asthma, anxiety neurosis or even alcoholism, but a detailed clinical 'cross-examination' reveals more often than not a disturbance of the love life.

This does not mean that a person in love will necessarily develop a neurosis, but it must be recognised that he or she is in a highly suggestible state akin to hypnosis.

Any idea introduced, if accepted, is likely to act with the force of a hypnotic suggestion. Thus even a coward may become a hero under the influence of love. If, however, the idea arouses a conflict in the mind, then a neurosis may result. It is well known from the work of Luria in Russia that a neurosis can be deliberately and experimentally produced by hypnosis. It is important to realise that neurosis may arise from accidental self-hypnosis, and it is, therefore, possible for it to occur when the mind is emotionally disturbed, as in love.

The following cases are typical.

Mr. ——, a married man of forty-five, reported with asthma. He imagined he must be 'allergic' to dust at work, as he was always worse there. Investigation revealed, however, that his 'sweater girl' typist was the real cause of the trouble. A guilty conscience concerning his infatuation created sufficient conflict and nervous tension to upset his breathing. Once he had experienced a spasm of 'asthma' the fear of further attacks kept them going.

A few sessions of hypnosis enabled him to take a more sensible view of things, and lose not only his asthma but his infatuation.

Mrs. —— suffered from 'migraine.' Her sick headaches were always worse when her husband was away on business. No wonder—she worried herself sick wondering what he was doing! Reluctantly she admitted she felt neglected and jealous, while she suspected her husband of seeking consolation elsewhere. The anxiety and nervous tension caused her headaches. Hypnosis, with explanation and reassurance, enabled her to see that her fears were groundless, with consequent relief from her headaches.

Mr.——, a single man of forty, complained of attacks of 'panic.' A history revealed that he had 'fallen in love' for the first time and desired to get married. Being a real 'mother's boy,' however, he 'panicked' at the idea of leaving Mother and taking on the responsibilities of marriage. A few sessions of hypnosis enabled him to make up his mind, pluck up his courage, take the plunge into matrimony and lose his 'panics.'

Mr. ——, a married man of forty-five, was an alcoholic. Investigation revealed that he had 'taken to drink' when his wife left him temporarily for another man during the war. Although she had come back, and they were now apparently happy together, he admitted having a constant feeling of anxiety lest they should be separated again. His excess drinking was an effort to subdue this anxiety. Hypnosis enabled him to see that he had no need to doubt his wife's loyalty now, and that alcoholism was probably the only thing which would drive her away again. As a result he soon lost his anxiety and found it easy to give up alcohol.

Mrs. ——, a married woman of about forty, complained of severe insomnia. Examination of her case revealed that it had started when she had felt attracted to a business acquaintance of her husband's. Although she had long ago overcome this temporary infatuation, she had continued to worry over the insomnia which it had provoked. The anxiety over this created nervous tension and kept the insomnia going. Hypnosis enabled her to relax, lose her fear of the condition, and sleep naturally.

These, and many similar cases, show that love and the emotional disturbances it creates is often the starting-point of many psychosomatic disorders.

In such cases ordinary advice is practically useless, for it literally 'goes in one ear and out of the other.' Everybody knows how hopeless it is to argue with a person in love! Hypnosis, however, by bringing about a superconcentration of the mind, enables suggestion to be absorbed to a much greater extent. This enables the medical man to approach these problems with greater advantage. A proper understanding of this subject may help medical men to:

Prevent unsuitable marriages by enabling those concerned to distinguish clearly between real love and mere infatuation.

Safeguard marriage and prevent divorce as the result of hasty, ill-considered decisions arising from emotional disturbance.

Deal with the vast army of those who have no real disease at all—merely 'nerves'—yet who comprise over 50 per cent of any general practice.

Chapter Seventeen

HYPNOSIS AND SEX

Is HYPNOSIS THE secret of sex appeal? Modern research in hypnotherapy would suggest that it is.

Successful treatment of many cases of sex disorders by hypnotherapy based on the theories presented here would seem to show how to attract the opposite sex by hypnosis. By hypnosis, of course, we mean hypnosis in the scientific sense— that is, a state of mind—not the usual hocus-pocus associated with the word in the lay mind.

Sex is generally regarded as being due to 'glands.' Glands, however, can work only in response to a nervous message. The original impulse must come from the mind. It is well known that the thought of food can make the mouth water—that is, make the salivary glands work. It is a matter of common knowledge that the sex organs and glands can be affected by thought. Scientists have proved experimentally that practically every organ can be influenced by hypnotic suggestion.* Treatment of sex disorders must therefore primarily be directed to the mind. It is of little use injecting gland extracts and hormones in cases which really need some good advice implanted firmly in the head.

Points concerning the stimulation of glands by thought are first:

Stimulation is by indirect suggestion

To make the salivary glands work the hypnotist does not merely say 'salivary glands work' or 'mouth water.' Instead he paints a word picture of appetising food. As the patient's mind absorbs the suggestion the appropriate message is sent to the salivary glands and the mouth waters. Second:

* Van Pelt, S. J., *Hypnotic Suggestion: Its Role in Psychoneurotic and Psychosomatic Disorders*, 35–36. John Wright & Sons Ltd., Bristol, 1955.

It must be the right suggestion

Suggestion of a 'blood-red steak' to a vegetarian would probably make him vomit, rather than make his mouth water. If a steak-eater were asked to think of a 'nice nut cutlet' or some other vegetarian dish, probably mere irritation would result. But let a steak-eater think of an appetising steak, and the mouth waters. It is a case of one man's meat is another man's poison.

These are two of the points which make hypnotherapy a job for the specialist. It is not good enough simply to know how to induce hypnosis. Finding the real cause of the trouble and deciding upon the right suggestions demands considerable knowledge and experience, and an entirely new and original conception of psychosomatic and psychoneurotic disorders.

Similar principles apply concerning sex. 'Vital statistics,' those magic figures 36–24–36, and 'cheese-cake' pictures can appeal to some men, but not to others.

'Mr. Beef-cake' and 'Mr. Muscles' may cause some bosoms to heave, while other women prefer the Yul Brynner haircut!

In abnormal cases men may provoke sex feelings in men, and women may attract members of their own sex.

Sex may even be stimulated by inanimate objects or certain rituals.

Whenever the sex glands are stimulated, with all the resultant complicated bodily and mental changes, it means that some person, thing or idea has captured the subject's mind and concentrated it sufficiently to implant an idea which has been fully absorbed.

Concentration, or rather superconcentration, of the mind is hypnosis. Any idea implanted in the mind at this time, unless it is definitely against the subject's fundamental moral code, will probably be accepted. Once accepted it acts with the force of a hypnotic suggestion, and the appropriate messages are sent to the organs and glands via the nervous system.

In the bad old days of stage hypnotism it was common to see a young man dancing with, or attempting to kiss, a broom, the suggestion having been planted in his mind that the broom was Greta Garbo or some luscious film blonde.

In real, everyday life we see almost as bizarre performances.

It is a commonplace to hear of some married couple 'What on earth did she see in him?' or 'He must have been blind when he married her!' 'Love is blind' is a well-known saying. This is only half true. Far from being blind, love sees even what is not there!

For instance, some young man may feel madly attracted to a girl and marry her, declaring to all the world she is an angel. Other people may point out that she is a lazy good-for-nothing, but it falls on deaf ears. Something about her has suggested to him that she is desirable, and he sees her as he imagines she is—that is, he is literally hypnotised.

In other words, the person with 'sex appeal' concentrates the attention of the one who is attracted deliberately or accidentally, and consciously or unconsciously implants the suggestion in the mind that he or she is the answer to that person's deepest wishes, whereas, in fact, the opposite may really be the case.

It is well known that emotion concentrates the mind into a condition akin to hypnosis. Emotional and romantic circumstances often accentuate the apparent appeal of the person with 'it.'

Even the best hypnotic subject, however, can break the trance if conditions become really intolerable—for instance if suggestions are made with which he fundamentally disagrees.

This explains why so many marriages go on the rocks.

When the victim finds that the reality of marriage is entirely unlike the picture which was suggested by the partner and his own imagination, then disillusionment follows. Strong emotion can destroy the previous hypnosis. Entirely opposite ideas can be implanted in a mind freshly concentrated into a new state of hypnosis, with the result that love can easily turn to hate.

Such disillusionment is particularly likely to result where people marry for rather superficial reasons, such as 'sex appeal.' Most film stars are frequently getting married and divorced; apparently they should make ideal couples—the men usually handsome and the women beautiful. Both usually have more than enough money to make anybody happy—yet divorce is the rule. Probably these people, living largely in an artificial, make-believe world, marry expecting things which no partner could live up to.

Very often the patient is referred to the hypnotherapist by his doctor not for any sexual disorder but for some ordinary symptom which disguises the underlying sexual tension.

General practitioners very often do not hear the whole truth in these matters. Very often the patient does not even realise that the symptom could be due to sex. Even when he does, embarrassment may prevent him from confiding his sexual troubles to the doctor he often regards as a personal friend or social acquaintance.

Records of many cases of asthma, migraine, insomnia, anxiety neurosis or 'panic attacks,' alcoholism and other nervous and allied disorders reveal that they have a sexual basis.

'Reluctant wives,' 'frustrated females,' 'inconstant nymphs,' 'men in despair,' 'queer types,' 'slaves of the fetish' and 'sex delinquents' feature high up on the list of those suffering from psychosomatic and psychoneurotic disorders.

The following typical cases show that hypnotherapy can help to solve sexual problems and dispel the attendant symptoms.

The Case of the Reluctant Wife

Mrs. —— was a very 'mixed-up Mrs.' She nursed an obsession for bald men. The trouble was her husband was tall, dark and handsome! The climax came when she suggested he should have a Yul Brynner haircut. Thinking of the boys at the office he refused, and she promptly had a breakdown. 'Panic attacks,' inability to think, asthma-like attacks and a host of nervous and allied complaints made life a misery for everybody— including her doctor. She had been advised by a psychiatrist to live apart from her husband.

Investigation revealed a very simple cause. She had always been deeply attached to her father, who was bald. At work she began to feel attracted to bald men. As the only ones she met were married, she felt panicky about doing anything wrong. Marriage, she thought, would be safe. Unfortunately, there being no bald man available, she married 'tall, dark and handsome.' Naturally the marriage was not a great success. Hypnotherapy, however, was able to convince her that bald-headed men no longer attracted her and that she could take more interest in her husband. This she did, made a success of her marriage and has had several children.

The Case of the Man in Despair

Mr. —— complained that his wife was too beautiful! Her 'vital statistics' gave him migraine and insomnia. The trouble was he just couldn't make love to her at all! Investigation revealed a curious obsession. He felt peculiarly attracted to any woman who was crippled. His reason, social and professional position had told him he should marry a charming, beautiful woman. His deepest emotional instincts, however, craved the company of a cripple. The nervous tension generated by this conflict rendered him impotent, and the worry of it caused migraine and insomnia.

The explanation was simple. At an early age his mother, a beautiful woman, found him indulging in some childish sex play with a little crippled girl. She punished him severely. His mind jumped to the conclusion—'crippled girl equals pleasure—beautiful woman equals punishment.' A few sessions of hypnotherapy were able to free the patient's mind of this foolish idea, and he was able to live a normal married life.

The Case of the 'Sex Kitten' who was Cold, or the Inconstant Nymph

Miss —— had a Marilyn Monroe figure, but her social life was about nil. The trouble was she suffered from 'petting panics.' Although she attracted men by the score she could never get any emotional feelings for them, and was repulsed by their advances. As a result she avoided social contacts more and more. She complained of feeling 'inferior,' 'frustrated' and 'unable to mix with people.'

The cause of her trouble was simple enough. She had hated and feared her father—a real tyrant. She could not bear him to touch her. He resented this and used to order her to sit on his knee, kiss him and show affection. The idea was implanted in her head that all men were hateful. Naturally, later on, when she began to attract men she found their attentions distasteful. Hypnotherapy enabled her to adjust her ideas, and some time later she was able to report that she was now living a normal social life, had a boy friend she really loved, and looked forward to getting married.

.   .   .   .   .

Doctors should consider the possibility of underlying sexual difficulties in many psychosomatic and psychoneurotic disorders such as migraine, asthma, insomnia and anxiety neurosis.

Where the history suggests a psychological cause, hypnotherapy should be tried first.

Patients who have any sexual difficulties should realise that these may be responsible for a multitude of symptoms and be quite frank, telling their doctors full details of any sexual difficulties.

Those who wish to attract the opposite sex should find out the likes and dislikes of the person it is desired to attract. Don't expect lasting harmony between a 'rock and roll' addict and a lover of opera or ballet.

See that suggestion by word or deed conforms to what the object of affection expects. It is no good buying two tickets for the fights if the loved one thinks boxing is brutal.

Self-examination is essential to make sure what is really wanted. Avoid pretence. It cannot be kept up. It is no good pretending to be the quiet, home- and country-loving type if a career and a gay social and town life represent Heaven.

Once decided, employ the principles of successful hypnotherapy. Concentrate the loved one's attention. Use imagination—paint a rosy picture of married life together. Remember certain situations are well known to predispose towards arousing emotion—moonlight, for instance.

Those already married should keep up the habits of their courting days. If not happy, they should do a bit of heart-searching and go back to them. It is never too late to mend!

Chapter Eighteen

HYPNOTHERAPY AND HOMOSEXUALITY

HYPNOTHERAPY CAN CURE homosexuals. It is probably the most effective treatment available to stem the rising tide of a vice which is already eight times more prevalent than it was twenty years ago. Homosexuals are made, not born. There are only two sexes; if a man finds women unattractive for any reason, then he naturally turns towards his own sex. Incomplete men may be interested in both.

Actual initiation is, of course, by corruption by an active homosexual, but a study of predisposing factors reveals that often a woman is to blame. Typical of cases in the records of this society is that of Mr. ——, a university student. His mother caught him at some childish sex play on occasions, and always punished him severely. This impressed on his mind the idea that a woman and sex did not go together. Men presented no such problems; therefore he became the easy prey of an established homosexual. Hypnotherapy enabled him to adjust his mind to the idea that he could have normal feelings for women and take no sexual interest in men.

Suggestion plays an important part. Mr. ——, a bank clerk, was rather weedy. As a youth he had always admired the strong bodies of other boys. His excessive shyness with girls made him unattractive to them. Reading a pseudo-scientific book on psychology, he jumped to the conclusion that he must be homosexual to think of men in this way. This frightened him, made him antisocial, and drove him into the society of homosexuals. Again, hypnotherapy enabled him to adjust his point of view and become normal.

Some of the most dangerous suggestions put forward today are that 'homosexuals are a race apart,' that 'they cannot help it,' that 'there is no cure' and that, in any case, 'there is no harm in it.' Gullible and suggestible young men absorb these foolish ideas, and become easy prey to the first pervert they meet.

Broadly speaking, a homosexual is nothing more or less than a man with a foolish idea in his head—that he likes men instead of women. Hypnotherapy can change ideas in this, as in other conditions. While it may be difficult to influence long-established, hard-bitten old sinners, it is certain that hypnotherapy can save any young man who wishes from a life of shame.

Chapter Nineteen

HYPNOTHERAPY AND SEX CRIME

THIS COUNTRY IS suffering from a considerable wave of sex crime; and while the police are actively concerned with catching the culprits the public is understandably asking what is being done to prevent these felonies.

By sex crimes are meant those described in the courts as indecent assault, rape and lust murder. The capital charge invariably hits the headlines, but it is obvious that for each of the lesser crimes that achieves the publicity of police court procedure a large number of cases must remain unreported for one reason or another.

The havoc wrought on the minds of the victims of these attacks is a factor which is probably not widely enough realised. Many may imagine the immediate state of unhappiness and despair. But through the years that follow may be built up perversions, neurosis and even criminal tendencies that are rarely traced back to the primary incident.

It is doubtful whether police organisations will ever be competent to deal with the prevention of psychopathic crime, for there is no routine approach to the problem.

The truth is that when the human mind is in a state of sexual turmoil there is no knowing what violent and antisocial acts may be perpetrated as a sort of outburst from conventional behaviour.

Reports received from members of the British Society of Medical Hypnotists who are called upon to deal with cases of sexual maladjustment in day-to-day practice indicate that the urge to commit sex crimes is rarely of sudden or unexpected incidence. It seems clear that the criminal potentiality is often built up over a long period of time behind a façade of social and domestic 'respectability.' Tendencies started by fears are often fostered by frustration.

It is when the mental and physical efforts of self-restraint break down and the social conscience of conventional behaviour is swamped that the sex urge takes complete control and a crime is committed.

The growing volume of case-histories at our command certainly suggests that medical hypnotherapists have prevented the commission of sex crimes when the potential criminals have been presented for treatment. As typical examples the following cases may be quoted.

Mr. ——, a thirty-year-old clerk, unmarried, was sent to a hypnotherapist for treatment because of lack of confidence, poor memory, fits of depression, inability to mix socially— especially with women—and an overwhelming fear of blood.

Under light, 'waking hypnosis,' the patient revealed fears that he might become a sex murderer. He found himself going out of his way to insult and hurt women verbally, and believed that at any moment his 'brain might snap' and that he might do physical injury.

Anxiety over these fears had provoked his symptoms, and the prime cause of the trouble was quickly revealed.

As a small boy he had been caught indulging in sex play with a little girl. His father had given him an unmerciful thrashing and threatened to 'kill him' if he ever touched a girl again.

Long after the incident had vanished from his conscious memory, the force of the parental instruction had persisted. As he grew up he shunned girls, though he naturally desired them; then he began to insult them. They were a menace to his peace of mind, and so grew the urge to do attractive women physical harm.

When he read of sex murders, he confessed, the urge to emulate them became frightening.

Fortunately, the patient responded well to a course of hypnotherapy; the fears of his childhood were resolved and his symptoms dispersed. He is now able to mix socially with women, and his attitude to sex is no longer abnormal.

Mr. ——, a forty-eight-year-old bank manager, married, persuaded his doctor to send him to a hypnotherapist for the treatment of insomnia. The patient was conscious that he had abnormal sex feelings, especially an urge to interfere with little girls. He would not confide in his doctor for social reasons—they played golf and bridge together!

The patient's abnormal feelings were resolved without undue difficulty by hypnotherapy.

In the above cases there can be little doubt that the patients were in grave danger of becoming criminal degenerates. And the happiness, if not the lives, of others was protected.

In view of what is now known about the motives that lead to the commission of sex crimes, it is logical and timely that urgent consideration should be given by the law to the treatment of such cases by the most effective methods available to modern medicine.

The recognition of this principle should serve to focus attention on means of preventive treatment rather than on the punishment of the criminal after the offence has been committed.

The value of modern methods of hypnotherapy is slowly but surely becoming recognised. That it can be used in the prevention of crime as well as in the treatment of psychoneuroses is being proved by a growing volume of evidence both in this country and abroad.

In view of the serious social problems presented by the rising tide of sex crimes, the Government should institute an immediate inquiry into the employment of hypnotherapeutic methods in the prevention of sex crime and the treatment of actual offenders.

Chapter Twenty

HYPNOTISM AND DIVORCE

HYPNOTISM CAN HELP doctors prevent divorces. Medical men are in an ideal position to detect the earliest signs of matrimonial trouble. Sex, perhaps the commonest cause of marital disharmony, frequently 'rears its ugly head' in the surgery. Unfortunately it often passes unnoticed. There are two main reasons. Firstly, it is frequently disguised. Asthma, migraine, insomnia, anxiety, 'panic attacks,' skin complaints and a host of other similar disorders are often only indications of underlying sexual tension.

Secondly, patients do not tell. General practitioners seldom hear the whole truth in these matters. This may be due to embarrassment, or simply that the patient does not realise the connection between marital disharmony and the complaint.

The following case illustrates these points.

The Case of the Reluctant Wife—or Asthma, not Passion

Mrs. ——, a young married woman, complained of severe asthma attacks. These started shortly after her marriage and prevented her living a normal married life. She feared that this might lead to a break-up of her marriage. Investigation revealed that she felt guilty, for religious reasons, for having married a divorced man. Nervous tension generated by worry had interfered with her breathing. Fear of the feelings experienced during her first asthma attack merely created more tension, and set up a vicious circle. Hypnotherapy, by inducing relaxation and dispelling tension, soon stopped her attacks. Suitable suggestion enabled her to lose her 'guilty' feeling and live a normal sex life. When asked why she had not discussed her sex life with her general practitioner, she said that she had never thought it could be connected with the asthma.

Another case, that of the woman who developed a rash

resulting from her husband's paying undue attention to other women, has been discussed in the chapter on Hypnosis and Beauty.

Patients can help doctors by realising that many symptoms such as asthma, insomnia, migraine and anxiety or 'panic' attacks may easily be the result of worry over marriage problems.

They should tell their general practitioner everything that has a possible bearing on their case, and avoid hiding important factors for fear of embarrassment.

Doctors will be able to help patients and, in many cases, prevent divorce by being on the look-out for marriage difficulties as a possible cause for psychosomatic symptoms such as migraine, asthma, insomnia and other similar conditions.

They should make special efforts to gain the patient's confidence and encourage him to 'tell all.'

They should also remember that ordinary advice usually goes in one ear and out of the other, and only a fraction is absorbed, and therefore try to employ the principles of hypnotic suggestion in dealing with problems involving emotional difficulties. Patients should be taught to relax and concentrate on the doctor's advice. Suggestions should be simple and positive. The appeal should be to the imagination rather than the will-power.

In difficult cases which do not respond to these simple 'first aid' measures doctors should consider specialised hypnotherapy. This is a simple psychotherapeutic procedure of proved efficacy which can influence a patient's way of thinking far more effectively than any other psychological method. It is particularly effective when emotional problems are involved.

Chapter Twenty-one

HYPNOTHERAPY AND CRUELTY TO CHILDREN

IN RECENT YEARS there has been an alarming increase in the number of cases of cruelty to children.

Only rarely is the person responsible properly described as habitually brutal or of low intelligence.

Too often the act of cruelty proves to be an isolated incident which shames, humiliates and degrades an otherwise exemplary character.

What exactly causes the sudden senseless outburst of fury that impels an apparently normal and decent adult to beat a little child black and blue?

There is overwhelming evidence in the case-histories known to the author that the answer is to be found in the accumulation of nervous tension inspired by particular fears.

An important proportion of these cases follows two patterns.

The husband who is afraid that his wife loves their child more than him; and the wife who fears another pregnancy, laying the blame for her ill health on the child she bore with difficulty.

Such fears, unreasoning and spurious though they may be, develop readily into anxiety neuroses; and with a rising spiral of despair the fear spills over into violent and uncontrollable physical action.

These neuroses respond readily to the modern technique of waking hypnosis.

It is not uncommon for medical hypnotherapists to have the opportunity of preventing a cruel attack upon an infant, for cases are on record where parents have anticipated such a peril and sought advice and treatment in time.

More often the patient is sent along with a case-history of 'panic attacks,' feelings of insecurity and dread, insomnia, and perhaps migraine or some other psychosomatic symptom.

It is then that the potential child-beater can often be identified, and the tragedy averted by suitable treatment.

Typical of case reports available is that of Mrs. ——. She was obsessed with the idea that she might lose control of herself and injure her little girl. Apparently she had nearly lost her life having the baby, and she had been told she would 'probably die' if she became pregnant again. Fear, worry and resentment built up such a pitch of nervous tension that she feared she would be unable to control herself. Waking hypnosis enabled her to relax, lose her nervous tension and see that her fears were really groundless. It is quite certain from reports of many similar cases that modern waking hypnosis could prevent many senseless outbursts of fury which result in revolting cases of cruelty to children.

Chapter Twenty-two

HYPNOTISM AND THE BACKWARD CHILD

IN THESE DAYS when its whole educational future may be decided at the age of eleven or so it is more essential than ever that a child should not be handicapped by emotional problems which prevent it from doing its best.

Many potentially brilliant children are held back by nervousness, over-anxiety and emotional problems which show little or no response to ordinary methods. Records available to this society show that modern hypnotherapy can often achieve brilliant results in this very important field.

The Case of Cinderella in the Classroom

Little Jane was unable to read. She refused to make any effort to learn. Investigation revealed that she had been badly frightened by a thoughtless teacher at her first school. Fear prevented her from concentrating or taking any interest in lessons. A few sessions of hypnotherapy freed her mind from fear and implanted a desire to read. Some time later her father wrote: 'Jane can now read perfectly and fluently. She can read at sight, and as quickly as a grown-up person. The headmistress of her school marvels at what she calls "the miracle," and last week Jane went from the bottom place in her class to the top.'

No other form of treatment could bring about such a transformation in only four weekly sessions in a little girl who previously could read only with hesitation, great difficulty and intense dislike.

We would, in all modesty, challenge any one of, or indeed all, those psychiatrists who are fond of denigrating hypnotism to deny the truth of this.

The Case of the Dunce who Never Was

John was so nervous that he did very badly at school. Investigation revealed that he had been badly frightened by a burglar as a child. As a result he suffered from nightmares, and was unable to concentrate properly on his work or games. A few weekly sessions of hypnosis removed his fears and restored his confidence. The following report indicates the success of the treatment.

'All his old nervousness has gone, and he now thoroughly enjoys his games. His powers of concentration have developed to such an extent that he is top of the "A" stream at school, the "A" stream led to a university.'

This transformation too was achieved in only a few weekly sessions.

In each case the father was a man of high intelligence and distinguished academic attainments. However, even in children of less gifted parents hypnotherapy, can bring out the very best of which they are capable.

It cannot, of course, 'make a silk purse out of a sow's ear.' Furthermore such results are brought about by using hypnotic suggestion scientifically in the modern manner. They cannot be expected to be achieved by naïve, out-of-date, hit-or-miss methods usually demonstrated by stage performers and amateurs.

All teachers and those in charge of children should realise the possibilities of modern scientific hypnotherapy for those in difficulty.

Chapter Twenty-three

CAN HYPNOTHERAPY PREVENT ROAD ACCIDENTS?

THERE WERE OVER a hundred thousand road casualties and more than two thousand deaths due to road accidents in Britain during the first six months of 1953. In all of them it is quite safe to say that some error of human judgment was responsible, for accidents do not 'just happen.' The problem is so serious that the matter has been discussed in Parliament, and various remedies suggested. As usual, each class of road user has sought to place the blame on the other. 'More severe penalties for motorists,' cry the cyclists. 'Stricter laws for cyclists,' demand the motorists. 'Fine the jay-walker,' they both suggest with enthusiasm. Even the Church enters the fray and the Archbishop of York was reported to have said that the number of road accidents would drop rapidly if the cars of dangerous drivers were confiscated!

Everybody is uniting in blaming the Government for not providing better roads. Politicians reply by suggesting stricter laws and more regulations for every class of road user!

It is submitted that the solution to this problem does not lie so much in simply building better roads or introducing more severe penalties or restrictions for road users as in tackling the fundamental problem of the mental processes of the 'accident-prone.'

It cannot be denied that even the worst accident black spots are negotiated quite safely by thousands, perhaps even millions, of people each year. Many accidents occur at speeds well within the limit and others take place under what might be termed ideal traffic conditions. It is obvious that the human element is involved, and if this could be dealt with adequately then casualties and deaths on the road would no doubt drop even without any alterations in the law or traffic conditions at all.

The hypnotherapist is often called upon to deal with cases that have failed to respond to more conventional treatments. And most of these 'incurables' prove to be accident-prone car drivers!

In addition, we are aware that some accidents are caused by mechanical failures beyond the driver's control, yet still related to the human element.

The Case of the Forgetful Motor Mechanic

Consider the case of Mr. ——, a young married motor mechanic who was sent for treatment. A typical ' neurotic,' he complained of insomnia, lack of concentration and confidence and a conscious feeling of nervous tension.

Recently he had jeopardised his job at the garage because he had failed properly to carry out brake adjustments on a car, and as a result the customer had narrowly escaped serious accident.

Since the onset of his symptoms he had been unable to take any real interest in his work. Apparently his insomnia had started while looking after his sick wife and child.

He continued to worry even after recovery, and symptoms of anxiety and preoccupation with his unpleasant feelings had led to the lack of concentration which might easily have resulted in a fatal road accident. A few sessions of hypnotherapy were sufficient to teach him to relax, to remove his dangerous symptoms and restore his confidence. It is impossible, however, not to wonder how many people there must be in responsible positions whose personal problems turn them into potential menaces to road users.

Alcohol, for instance, is well recognised as such a serious menace that the drunken driver is liable to severe penalties. How many people take alcohol or drugs such as phenobarbitone or amytal in quantities which while stopping short of intoxication, nevertheless turn them into dangerous drivers?

If the figures for nervous patients, the consumption of alcohol and the quantity of phenobarbitone prescribed in Britain are any criterion, then such people must contribute materially to the incidence of road accidents.

The Case of the 'Panicky' Driver

Mr. ——, a middle-aged married man and a commercial traveller, complained of attacks of 'panicky feelings' which were especially liable to come on while driving in heavy traffic. He had got into the habit of taking increasing doses of pheno-barbitone and alcohol to ward off these attacks. The dents and scratches on his car testified to a number of minor errors of judgment, and the patient stated that he was afraid to drive much more for fear of a serious accident. And without a car he would lose his job.

During a course of hypnotherapy he was able to trace the cause of his fears to a car accident when learning to drive. After several sessions he was able to regain his confidence, laugh at all his old fears and give up alcohol and drugs.

It is obvious that such treatment, besides its immediate beneficial effects on the patient, must have saved him and probably other people from being involved in a serious if not fatal accident.

The Case of the Henpecked Motorist

The aggressive driver is one of the greatest menaces on the road. Such a person, if temporarily baulked or obstructed in any way, may take the most foolhardy risks to 'beat the other fellow' and 'show him who is the better driver.'

Mr. —— was such a man. Nagged at home by his wife, brow-beaten by his boss at the office, and haunted by a sense of inferiority because of his small stature, he seethed with inward resentment and longed to 'take it out of somebody.'

At the wheel of the car, he gave free rein to his feelings and literally set out to 'blast people off the road.' He came for treatment because of his feelings of inferiority, lack of confidence and uncontrollable outbursts of temper while driving. He would actually shout and swear at other drivers. This once earned him a black eye, for he was ill suited to physical combat, and he realised himself that he was a menace on the roads. Hypno-therapy eventually enabled him to adjust himself to his cir-cumstances, and his treatment no doubt prevented yet another addition to the toll of the road.

Such behaviour is not, of course, confined exclusively to the motorist. The aggressive pedestrian who demands his 'rights' and thinks a bus can pull up dead in a couple of feet on a slippery, wet road just because he puts his foot on a zebra-crossing is well known. Either he finishes up in hospital or the bus skids, and, perhaps, kills or injures half a dozen innocent people.

The Case of the ex-P.O.W. Mentality

Few road users come in for so much criticism as motor cyclists. Owing to the tremendous power, speed and manoeuvrability of their machines, motor cyclists—especially youthful riders—are often tempted to take foolish risks, so that they figure very largely in any table of road accident figures.

So generally is this recognised that the Government has considered making it compulsory for motor cyclists to wear crash helmets, or 'skid lids.' No amount of protective clothing, however, could have saved the following patient from being involved in a serious accident eventually.

Mr. ——, a young electrician and motor cyclist, was sent for treatment because he had an unfortunate spasm which caused him to jerk his head round as though to look behind him at the most unexpected moments. The origin of this habit was soon brought to light as the result of hypnotherapy. He had been a prisoner of war and had escaped. Fear of capture had caused him constantly to look over his shoulder to see if he was being followed, and the habit persisted long after the war had been almost forgotten. As it was linked by association of ideas with anxiety, it was most likely to occur at times of stress. Strangely enough the patient had never thought that it might prove dangerous while riding a motor cycle at speed, yet it needed only an unfortunate combination of circumstances for the spasm to divert his attention at a critical moment and the road would have claimed at least one more victim. Fortunately a course of hypnotherapy was able to remove his trouble, but there must be many people whose peculiar habits make them a danger on the road.

The Case of the Nervous Cyclist

No age limit is set, so that it is not unusual to see quite young children wobbling about perilously in heavy traffic on cycles quite unsuitable for them. There is no test to pass and no examination in the Highway Code, so that anybody who can manage to afford a bicycle is free to use the roads, even if he puts himself and others in peril by his carelessness. Plenty of people whose nervous disabilities or physical defects make them potential menaces are regularly cycling about the roads of Britain today.

Mr. ——, a young single man, was such a one. He complained of attacks of anxiety, lack of concentration, poor memory and occasional 'black-outs.' These he described as 'dizzy feelings' with 'palpitations of the heart,' 'sinking feelings' in the stomach and 'everything going black' for a moment or two. Inquiry revealed that in spite of these alarming symptoms he rode a bicycle to work regularly and had had several narrow escapes in traffic with his 'bad turns.' It had not occurred to him to give up riding his cycle!

During the course of treatment by hypnotherapy it was revealed that he had been knocked off his bicycle by a motor-car as a child and, although not seriously hurt, had been badly frightened. He had quite forgotten this incident of childhood until it was recalled by hypnosis. A course of treatment was sufficient to clear up his fears and anxieties and, in doing so, no doubt saved another potential victim of the road.

For every such patient the hypnotherapist meets in practice there must be thousands of other people whose nervous fears, anxieties and habits make them potential menaces on the road, be they motorists, motor cyclists, cyclists or pedestrians.

Prevention, of course, is better than cure, and the ideal thing would be for people with nervous and allied complaints to have them removed before venturing into the 'hurly-burly' of modern traffic conditions.

If general practitioners recognised the potential danger of these nervous patients and sent them for hypnotherapy instead of simply prescribing drugs such as phenobarbitone or amytal, then undoubtedly the figures for road accidents would decrease rapidly.

Children, for instance, who always make good hypnotic subjects, could be trained by a few simple suggestions *always* to take care in traffic and observe the necessary precautions quite automatically. 'Learner' drivers could have their confidence greatly increased, to the obvious benefit of themselves and others.

While it may not be possible to persuade everybody concerned to co-operate voluntarily in this way, at least where an accident has occurred the law could demand that those involved should be examined to see if any nervous condition had been responsible. If so, it could be made a condition that the person responsible should have to undergo a course of approved treatment before he was allowed to resume use of the road. After all, four or six weeks' treatment by hypnotherapy to cure an alcoholic driver is much better than sending him to prison, confiscating his driving licence and losing him his position.

In order to conform to the demands of modern life it is essential that the treatment should be relatively quick, with the minimum of inconvenience, loss of time and money both to the community and the individual. Under these conditions hypnotherapy is obviously the most suitable method.

Chapter Twenty-four

HYPNOSIS AND GENIUS

THIS CHAPTER MIGHT almost be entitled 'How to be a Genius.'
Modern research in hypnosis has revealed the secret of genius;
further it has demonstrated that it may be possible for a person
of average ability to develop positive genius under the influence
of hypnosis. This is no Svengali-Trilby story, but cold scientific
fact.

Consider that under the influence of hypnotic suggestion an
artist painted a picture in six hours which would have normally
taken seventy hours. Furthermore, it was a picture that he had
tried to paint unsuccessfully for ten years,* and that in Chapter
12 we saw that when Rachmaninoff found himself unable to
compose, hypnotic treatment by Dr. Dahl of Moscow enabled
him to complete his concerto and achieve great success.

Admittedly there are degrees of genius. Not everybody can
be a Rachmaninoff or an Einstein. Nevertheless, hypnotic
research shows that most people can be much better than they
are. Hypnosis can reveal the brains that most people have, but
have not even used yet! Hypnosis cannot 'make a silk purse out
of a sow's ear'; it can, however, enable a person to make the
most of the brains that he possesses. Most people have the
potentiality for genius once the brake is removed.

Edison said: 'Genius is one per cent inspiration and ninety-
nine per cent perspiration.' Disraeli insisted that 'patience is a
necessary ingredient of genius.' 'Genius is an infinite capacity
for taking pains' is a well-known quotation. Evidence shows
that these sayings are only partly right. Many people work
exceedingly hard, but genius and success elude them.

Experience with hypnosis shows .that genius is the result
of the ability to superconcentrate the mind, and so make use of

* Cooper, Linn F., M.D. and Erickson, Milton H., M.D. *Time Distortion in
Hypnosis*, Part II, 164. The Williams & Wilkins Company, Baltimore, U.S.A., 1954.

practically all the mind power available. When all its resources are mobilised, the human brain is capable of the most fantastic feats.

Jed Buxton, the calculating marvel of 1749, could easily give the answer to such a simple problem as to how many peas could be contained in 202,608,000,260 cubic miles.

Alexander Murray, a poor Scottish shepherd boy, taught himself so many languages that he was eventually given the Chair of Oriental Languages at Edinburgh University in 1812.

Einstein, the father of relativity, was able in 1953 to concentrate his ideas into a single 'law' to explain all the workings of the Universe!

Any average person is a potential genius; anatomically there is no difference between the brain of the average person and the greatest genius. Both have approximately 10,000 million 'grey matter' brain cells. There is, however, a vast difference in the way they use them!

Brain-wave tests carried out on Einstein confirm the theory that genius is associated with the ability to superconcentrate the mind. They showed that he seemed to be able to focus an exceptionally large number of different groups of brain cells on any problem that he wished to consider deeply.

Superconcentration of the mind is the most reasonable explanation that we have of hypnosis. It is the only one which can satisfactorily account for the phenomena obtainable. It is well known that under the influence of hypnosis the mental faculties can be greatly increased to a level approaching genius. The patient can, for instance, recall memories of things completely forgotten in ordinary life.

The power of the mind can be increased by concentration under hypnosis in the same way as the whole body strength can be increased. The familiar phenomenon of general rigidity whereby even a frail subject can support the weight of a heavy man is well known. It would seem reasonable to assume that so-called natural genius is really a form of hypnosis—self-hypnosis brought about by superconcentration as the result of intense interest.

Tennyson, for instance, used to induce a kind of 'waking trance' by repeating his name silently to himself, and Coleridge claimed that he wrote 'Kubla Khan' in ecstasy, without his conscious knowledge.

The best hypnotic subjects are perfectly normal, highly intelligent people with great powers of imagination and concentration. Nervous, scatterbrained people with poor powers of concentration make poor hypnotic subjects. With training, as nervous patients become better and better subjects, their powers of concentration and mental powers improve out of all recognition.

In deep hypnosis, with 100 per cent concentration, the subject takes no notice of other things. The typical genius, concentrating on his pet subject, is oblivious to distractions. The absent-minded professor is a well-known figure.

Emotion, by concentrating the mind, favours the onset of hypnosis—particularly self-hypnosis. Genius is frequently associated with emotion, as in acting, painting or music.

Imagination is an essential factor in the production of hypnosis. Imagination is a prominent feature of genius.

Genius can be inhibited, or even destroyed, by circumstances which profoundly influence the mind, as in the case of Rachmaninoff, who lost the ability to compose because he was upset by the failure of his First Symphony at St. Petersburg in 1897.

Emotional disturbances can concentrate the mind into a condition of hypnosis. If frightening or disturbing ideas are introduced at the time, unpleasant symptoms are likely to accompany them. The patient's mind becomes more and more concentrated on his condition. A vicious circle is established and the mind power is wasted. If the vicious circle can be broken by hypnotherapy, the patient's mind power is freed for better things.

It is obvious that the opportunities to study a Rachmaninoff or an Einstein are few. Nevertheless, experience with quite ordinary cases shows that hypnotherapy can neutralise the ill effects of disturbing influences and enable the patient to make the most of his mental ability. Consider the following cases.

The Case of the Frustrated Fiddler

Unlike Nero, Peter 'burnt' while he fiddled. Investigation revealed that he had developed resentment as a child at the enforced practice which stopped him enjoying life like the other boys. As a result, he was a very frustrated fiddler, and had got nowhere in the musical world; he worried over this and developed insomnia. Some time after a short course of hypnotherapy he wrote to say that he now enjoyed playing, had obtained a position as leader of an orchestra, and slept perfectly.

The Case of the Agitated Actor

Roger was a very agitated actor. He suffered from stage fright in front of the camera, which resulted in a facial twitch. As a result he could see no future, and this anxiety made it worse. Hypnotherapy gave him confidence, with the result that he soon lost his facial twitch and did very well.

The Case of Painless Childbirth for Father

James, a young married man, was unable to study for his accountancy examinations. Investigation revealed that he had been badly upset when his wife nearly died after a difficult first childbirth. He worried himself sick in case they had another child. As a result his work went to pieces and he developed migraine. Hypnotherapy enabled him to overcome his fears and dispelled his migraine. His wife had her second baby quite painlessly under the influence of hypnosis, and the birth was painless for father too! With his mind free from worry, James passed his examinations with flying colours and soon obtained a very good position.

The cases described above, and many similar ones, show that *scientific* hypnotherapy can remove disabilities and enable patients to make the most of their mental powers. While hypnosis cannot guarantee a win on a television quiz show, or produce a race of super 'eggheads,' it is possible that it might be used, for instance, in selected cases, to produce the brilliant scientific geniuses who will be so much in demand in the coming Atom Age. 'Schools for Genius Training' might well be established in the future for bright students whose powers could be increased greatly by hypnosis.

Chapter Twenty-five

HYPNOSIS AND SPACE TRAVEL

> 'Almost every great step in the history of science, has been made by the "anticipation of nature," that is by invention of hypotheses which, although verifiable, often had very little foundation to start with.'
> *T. H. Huxley.*

IT IS HIGHLY probable that the first man on the moon will be hypnotised. Those who smile sceptically should remember that space travel is already with us. The Douglas Sky-rocket plane has carried its pilot, very briefly it is true, into the fringe of outer space. 'Arabella,' a rhesus monkey, has been hurled into space thirty-four miles above the earth by rocket and returned unharmed. Mice have been rocketed into space without, apparently, any ill effects.*

The medical problems involved are considered to be more formidable than the technical. So well recognised is this that a full-scale Department of Space Medicine has been established in the United States. From experiments conducted with animals carried into space by rockets it would seem that physically man should be able to stand the enormous stresses and strains involved.

Some idea of what these may be can be gained from the fact that a fourteen stone man will find his weight increased up to *half a ton* by the tremendous acceleration within a couple of minutes of taking off. As soon as the motors cut out and the space-ship is falling freely he will weigh nothing at all! Medical men concerned with the study of space travel are agreed, however, that the greatest problems will be psychological.

No doubt space-ships will be fitted with all possible automatic devices, but ultimately man will be in final control, and men twenty-five, fifty, a hundred or even a thousand years hence will have the same nervous systems as they have today. They

* Since writing this Russia has in fact successfully launched satellites into outer space.

will, no doubt, have perfected a better means of controlling them, and more than likely this will be by hypnosis. Mere cost alone, apart from other considerations, will make it imperative that the success of the first real space trip is not jeopardised by the failure of the human element.

Although there is already a considerable literature on space medicine, the author is unaware of any mention of the use of hypnosis in this connection. Yet with some of the main problems admitted to be psychological it is difficult to see how hypnosis can be overlooked. Considering merely the physical side of the question, there are obvious possibilities for the use of hypnosis. It is almost a matter of common knowledge and observation that even a frail youth can stiffen his muscles into a state of general rigidity under the influence of hypnotic suggestion. In this condition he can support the weight of, say, two or three people standing upon him while he is stretched between two supports—head on one, feet on the other. Such striking exhibitions always used to form a part of any stage demonstration. What has happened in a case such as this? The subject has merely used the full strength of his muscles.

Experience with electro-convulsant therapy has shown that the human muscles have more power than is generally supposed, and that by contracting violently they can even break bones. This fact accounted for the occasional fractures which occurred during electro-convulsant therapy before the use of drugs such as curare. In the normal, ordinary state the mind imposes a restriction, so that only a fraction of the real muscular strength is used. If asked to perform a feat, such as that described above, in the ordinary state the subject would have grave doubts of his ability to do so. As a result the mind power would be scattered, so that nothing like the full strength available would be used. In hypnosis the mind is concentrated and a more powerful message is sent to the muscles. As a result they exert all their force and appear to be fantastically strengthened.

In space travel, where the violent acceleration in the first few minutes will build up a pressure of, say, half a ton on the human frame, the advantage of hypnosis as a method of strengthening the space traveller is obvious. But, useful as hypnosis may be for assisting the spaceman physically, it is undoubtedly in the psychological realms that its greatest potentialities are to be found. While it is obviously impossible to quote actual cases showing the influence of hypnosis on space travellers, many of the conditions to which spacemen will have to adjust themselves mentally are not only known but have their counterparts in everyday life on this planet, as the following points show.

The Problem of Breathing Difficulties

It is known that the violent acceleration during the take-off will increase the weight of the space traveller so much that the chest will be held as in a vice. Breathing will be impossible for approximately twenty seconds during the first stage and up to forty seconds during the next. Obstruction to breathing is likely to cause panic in even the bravest man, and panic itself can further interfere with breathing.

Hypnosis will be invaluable in enabling future spacemen to face this ordeal without fear. How do we know this? Well, here on earth, many cases of asthma, for instance, know what it is like to feel the chest 'held as if in a vice.' Quite often the asthma itself is the result of panic arising from a temporary upset of the breathing, as the following case shows.

Mr. ——, a middle-aged married man, complained of severe attacks of asthma. He dreaded going to sleep at night, for he would always wake up gasping for breath. The attacks started after his wife had put a pillow over his face one night to stop him snoring! The patient dreamt he was being suffocated and woke up panic stricken. Fear of this feeling created tension and spasm which resulted in asthma. Hypnotism enabled him to lose his fear of breathlessness, relax and sleep naturally.

The Problem of Weightlessness

The moment the rocket motors cut out and the space-ship is coasting in space its passengers will lose all weight! They will have the most unpleasant sensation of falling into a bottomless pit. Instinctive efforts to save themselves from falling would result in their being violently thrown about, for the human muscles would be incredibly powerful in a state of weightlessness. Space travellers could be trained by hypnosis how to react to these conditions. It is well known that in hypnosis a subject can be taught to feel anything suggested. Thus it is quite common to suggest that a subject's arm is getting 'lighter and lighter' and will 'float' up in the air. In a good subject the arm will rise steadily. Again it is quite common for a hypnotised subject to feel as if he were 'floating.' Needless to say, he does not really float (in spite of the stories one hears about levitation!), but the patient nevertheless 'feels' the same as if he actually did. Sensations of 'floating' or 'falling' are quite common even in ordinary sleep. Consider the following case.

Mr. ——, a young single man, complained of frequent nightmares. He was an ardent enthusiast for space travel and devoured all the literature he could find on the subject. Practically every night he set out for the moon or Mars in his dreams, but inevitably he crash landed and woke up on the bedroom floor! When he dreamt he was falling in space he thrashed about so much he usually fell out of bed! Under hypnosis it was suggested that, if he had such a dream, he would enjoy the sensation of falling, let himself go relaxed and become used to it while imagining himself moving about his dream space-ship the way his heroes did in the films. The patient was vastly pleased with the result, and reported that now he could really enjoy his nocturnal space trips without falling out of bed!

The Problem of Nervous Strain

It is unlikely that men selected to man the first space-ship will be weaklings either mentally or physically. Nevertheless it would be wise to employ hypnosis as an insurance against the possibility of nervous breakdown under the extraordinary strains which will be imposed. Even on terra firma breakdowns occur in the most unexpected cases. The following case illustrates how a breakdown in the human element can jeopardise even the most important project.

Dr. —— was a brilliant young scientist. Secret experiments connected with military operations demanded that he should be left alone in an extremely desolate spot far from civilisation. At the last moment he was overcome with an attack of 'panic'— the 'screaming heebie-jeebies,' he called it—at the idea of being left alone and had to be relieved of his post. This entirely unsuspected weakness, a 'hangover' from childhood fears, was corrected by hypnosis, and he later carried out his task with complete satisfaction to all concerned. A space-ship will be unable to return to have its pilot, navigator or other members of the crew treated for neurosis! Therefore, more than likely, hypnosis will be used prophylactically to prevent any such breakdowns in personnel.

The Problem of Sleep

With the extraordinary sensations of weightlessness and the constant feeling of falling, spacemen are going to find it difficult, if not impossible, to sleep. Drugs would be contra-indicated as they might impair other faculties, so that hypnosis would seem to be the only means of ensuring adequate rest. The human body normally does not take kindly to changes in routine, and disturbance of sleep is common even in our humdrum earthly life. This is illustrated by the following case.

Mr. ——, a middle-aged business man, suffered from severe insomnia. This began when he had to start travelling a lot by land, air and sea. Hypnosis enabled him to sleep quickly whenever he wished, whether in a plane, ship or train, and disregarded any strange sensations to which his body might be subjected.

The Problem of Space Sickness

The extraordinary confusion of sensations pouring into the spaceman's brain as the result of the fantastic conditions of space travel will probably cause 'space sickness.' Here on earth we are familiar with travel sickness of various kinds. Seasickness, for instance, can prostrate the strongest man, and even some Commandos were laid low by it during the war. If severe, 'space sickness' could jeopardise any space project, and here again, as drugs may have undesirable side-effects, hypnosis is likely to be the method of choice to prevent such a catastrophe.

Captain —— was like Nelson—every time he went to sea he was seasick and found this most embarrassing. A course of hypnosis enabled him to overcome his difficulty with ease.

The Problem of Boredom

It is estimated that a trip round the moon may take only ten days. A round trip to Mars, however, is likely to last at least two or three years. Imagine being cooped up in a tiny cabin with two or three companions for such a time. Two or three years of weightlessness, the discomfort of space suits, artificial air and other abnormal conditions would be enough to try the nerves of even the strongest man. Hypnosis is an obvious way of making such conditions endurable. Cooper and Erickson* have shown that it is possible to produce time-distortion in hypnosis. By this means it should be possible to make even the most tedious journey appear to pass quickly and pleasantly without impairing in any way the efficiency of the crew of the space-ship. Even on earth similar problems are encountered.

Mr.——complained of a feeling of intense boredom and frustration. He stated he had a strong desire to 'run away from it all.' A well-paid but extremely boring job was the cause of his trouble. Owing to the good money he received (and the fear of what his wife would say!) he did not want to give it up. The work consisted of doing a very simple thing over and over. The patient had no interest in the job and he felt it all the worse because he had to work through the night alone. Under hypnosis it was suggested that the hours would simply seem to fly away, but, in spite of this, he would do his work conscientiously and well.

After a few treatments the patient reported himself delighted with the results. He said that he no sooner started work than it seemed to be time to go home again; in fact he had never known time to fly so fast!

In these and many other ways it is obvious that hypnosis would be able to help any future space travellers. It may be objected that all the cases quoted were very firmly established on earth and that conditions in space would be entirely different. For practical purposes, however, the human nervous system involved in these 'feelings' and 'sensations' appears to be incapable of telling the difference between a real thing and an imaginary one.

Thus the mere thought of food can make the mouth water just as much as if real food were offered. The mere suggestion of a near accident in a car can make the heart beat as rapidly as if the accident were real. The author† has published research

* Cooper, Linn F., M.D. and Erickson, Milton H., M.D., *Time Distortion in Hypnosis*. The Williams & Wilkins Company, Baltimore, U.S.A.; Baillière, Tindall & Cox Ltd., London, 1954.

† Van Pelt, S. J., 'The Control of the Heart Rate by Hypnotic Suggestion,' *Experimental Hypnosis* (Ed. Lecron). Macmillan, New York, 1952.

on the influence of hypnotic suggestion on the heart rate. To the nervous system the sensations evoked by the space traveller in dreams are just as real as if he were actually travelling in space. It is reasonable to suppose, therefore, that hypnosis, which is so useful on terra firma, will prove equally valuable to the future pioneers in the realms of space.

Chapter Twenty-six

NERVOUS EXHAUSTION

MRS. —— SEEMED to be in a bad way. According to her doctor she had suffered from complete mental and physical exhaustion for the last five years. In addition she complained of severe headaches—'like a tight band around the head'—insomnia, irritability, lack of concentration, failing memory and depression.

The exhaustion was so great that frequently she would be confined to her bed for weeks at a time, and when she arrived for consultation she had to be carried from the car.

Her doctor stated that she had been examined by numerous specialists and that all investigations had proved there was nothing organically wrong.

As Mrs. —— related her story, the nature of her condition soon became clear. Apparently she had been perfectly well and happy when she married at about the age of twenty-four. There seemed to be no indications of previous nervous trouble in either the patient or her family, apart from the fact that she admitted she had always been inclined to be jealous.

When she married, this jealousy seemed to centre itself around her husband. If he came home a little late she would accuse him of flirting with the girls in his office. Should he so much as glance at another woman, she would fly into a jealous temper. Things came to a head one day when she discovered some lipstick on his collar and felt convinced that he was having an affair with some woman or other. In vain did he protest that one of the fellows at the office must have put the lipstick on his collar for a joke. As it turned out later, this was quite true, for they all knew at the office how jealous she was.

However, at the time Mrs. —— had worked herself up into a state of hysterics, and said she thought she must have had a 'brainstorm.' According to her, she was in a terrible state, hardly slept a wink for a week, and suffered from such a bad headache that she 'felt her head would burst.' She felt she wanted to leave her husband one minute and the next she was afraid of breaking up her marriage and losing him.

With her mind being pulled in two opposite directions, it was no wonder that Mrs. —— felt as if 'her head would burst.'

However, she was quick to add that she felt that this unpleasantness could not be the cause of her present trouble, as she had long ago found out that her husband had been telling the truth and that there was no 'other woman.' In fact, she said they would be very happy together now were it not for her terrible exhaustion, which made it impossible to live a normal married or social life.

In spite of her doubts, however, Mrs. —— had to admit that all her difficulties seemed to follow this upset.

It was explained to her that now her condition was one of nervous exhaustion as the result of constantly holding herself tense—ready 'to fight or run away' as it were. Now it was the fear of her condition which created abnormal tension and so continued to exhaust her. Nevertheless there was some frightening idea which had started this tension and eventually led to the vicious circle of anxiety, tension and nervous exhaustion. It was easy enough to see that she had been considerably upset by her jealous fears, but there was something more frightening, which she was unable to remember now, to account for her serious condition.

She was told that her mind was too upset at the moment to remember the real trouble, but that, as she learned to relax, she would be able to think more clearly and the memory of what had frightened her would come into her mind without effort.

At the first hypnotic session Mrs. —— was taught how to relax, and at the next, a week later, she was told under light hypnosis that she would remember quite well the idea which had really frightened her.

When she reported for the third session a week later, Mrs. —— was all smiles. She said that she knew now what had really terrified her. At the time of the original trouble with her head 'bursting' she had felt as if she would go mad. In fact she admitted that she had thought she was mad. In her excited imagination she saw herself being confined in a mental home and this idea—the fear of insanity—had been introduced at a time of emotional crisis when her mind had been concentrated into a condition identical with hypnosis. As a result she had gone on being frightened, and the tension had resulted in extreme exhaustion. As her mind became more and more occupied with her symptoms, she had forgotten the original cause of her fear.

During the third session of light hypnosis it was pointed out to Mrs. —— that now she understood the cause of her trouble she could give up being afraid of it. She was no longer the jealous young wife of five years ago, so she no longer needed her feelings. In fact, now that she could relax and dispel her nervous tension, she would soon feel her strength returning.

A week later when she reported for her fourth session, Mrs. —— stated that already she felt 'on the mend.' At this session she was encouraged to form pictures in her mind—seeing herself like an actress on the screen in her imagination, and always picturing herself as she wanted to be—happy and cheerful, strong and well. The fifth and sixth sessions were directed to reinforcing these suggestions and others to a like effect, so that the patient would be able to face her problems in an adult manner instead of acting like a frightened, jealous child. After the sixth session Mrs. —— stated that she had been able to go out alone for the first time for five years, and that she now felt she would be able to enjoy life once more. Two years later she wrote to say that she was quite well.

Chapter Twenty-seven

ANXIETY NEUROSIS

'MR. ———,' WROTE his doctor, 'is a decent young fellow—thirty years of age and engaged to be married. He served in submarines during the war, but, although he had one or two narrow escapes, he suffered no injury of any kind and left the Service apparently quite fit at the end of hostilities. Since his return to civilian life, however, he has suffered from attacks of panic. These come on apparently for no reason at all, and he feels as if he is going to faint. He has been worried about his heart, but an electrocardiograph shows it to be perfectly normal. All other investigations show that organically he is perfectly fit. I think his condition must be nervous in origin.'

As Mr. ——— told his story the following facts emerged. Apparently he had always been 'a bit nervous' as a lad, although he could not say in exactly what way. He had served in the Navy during the war, having volunteered for submarine service, and on several occasions he admitted that he had been frightened. Cooped up in the submarine he had felt that others could see he was afraid, although nobody had ever suggested such a thing and his Service reports were excellent. On his return to civilian life he began to notice that he disliked crowds of people. Once, when dining with a girl friend, he had suddenly been seized with a terrible fit of panic. His heart had thumped, his face went red, he broke into a profuse perspiration, and finally blacked out. He felt that he had made a terrible fool of himself in front of the girl in a crowded restaurant and he had avoided such places ever since. Now he always felt ill at ease with people and could not go to social gatherings, dances, cinemas, theatres, restaurants or any of the usual places frequented by a young man of his position. It was becoming increasingly difficult for him to hold his position, as these senseless attacks of panic made him appear so foolish. In his own words, he got 'butterflies in the stomach' every time he saw the boss, and he had a constant feeling that he was being watched by others.

At the end of his story Mr. —— confessed that he was completely mystified as to why he should get these senseless attacks. Therefore it was explained to him that now he was afraid of these 'panicky attacks' and that as fear of any kind gave rise to the same 'feelings' of fear it was really this that was keeping his condition going. However, something had given rise to his original attack of panic, and it seemed to be connected with people. Therefore people must represent or remind him of some kind of danger which could give rise to fear and 'feelings of panic.'

There was one very likely cause, of course, in his wartime experiences. Often he had felt afraid when cooped up in the submarine and had sometimes thought that the others might see that he was afraid. That would be one very obvious reason for not liking people to look at him.

Mr. —— agreed that such thoughts had crossed his mind, but he insisted that it seemed to him the real fear was connected with people looking at him. He had often excused himself by thinking that the others in the submarine were probably just as frightened as he was, but he still could not get over his dislike of being looked at.

It was obvious that there was something deeper troubling Mr. ——, so he was told not to worry himself trying to think what had caused the trouble, as the memory of this would come back without any effort as he learned to relax and his brain became calmer. Well, after Mr. —— had practised relaxing for himself for a week or so after instruction under light hypnosis, he was given the suggestion during a session that he would remember quite well what had first caused him to dislike people looking at him.

A week later Mr. —— reported that 'a thought had just flashed into his head when he wasn't expecting it,' and related the following interesting story. Apparently his people had been quite wealthy and lived in a big old country manor house. This had many long dark passages which were lined with portraits of ancestors. If he had been naughty Mr. —— was told as a little boy that his famous ancestors would have strongly disapproved.

In fact they would probably turn in their graves if they knew how badly he had behaved. Furthermore, it was not at all certain that they were not even now regarding him with strong disapproval from the celestial regions.

He would be sent off to bed, and as he traversed the long dark corridors each portrait would be dimly illuminated in turn by the flickering light of the candle he carried. Mr. —— remembered being terrified on many occasions. He had the feeling that as he walked past the portraits of his distinguished ancestors their eyes followed him with strong disapproval of his naughtiness. Above all, he had been taught, the greatest sin was to be a coward.

'Well,' said Mr. ——, as he finished reciting this tale, 'it's a damned silly story, isn't it? I can see now why I don't like people looking at me, but I wonder why this childish fear took so long to come out?'

There is always the last straw that breaks the camel's back, it was explained to Mr. ——. If a man gets kicked by a horse he is usually careful of a horse next time. Should he be kicked a second time by a horse he will probably avoid going down the same street as a horse. If by any bad luck he should be kicked a third time he would probably decide a horse was a dangerous animal, shut himself up, refuse to go out and a psychoanalyst would say he had an 'obsession' or 'phobia' about horses. Actually all he would really have would be a very silly way of regarding and approaching a really delightful animal!

Mr. —— had in fact had three good kicks.

First of all, as a child traversing the long dark corridors, his mind had been concentrated on the idea that in certain circumstances people looking at him, although only painted ancestors, and the feeling of fear were linked together.

Later on, when cooped up in a submarine and expecting to be blown sky high at any moment by a depth charge, the very natural feelings of fear brought with them the associated idea of people looking at him. Later, in a crowded restaurant, the idea that people were looking at him automatically brought the feelings of fear. Having made a fool of himself by 'blacking out' the fear of doing this again in the presence of people was enough to set up a vicious circle. He had literally hypnotised himself into thinking he would have a panic attack if people looked at him.

In the course of several hypnotic sessions Mr. —— was taught that he could relax and feel at ease with people. It was pointed out that he was no longer a frightened little boy or a nervous young man in a submarine and that in future he would not care two hoots whether people looked at him or not. He was encouraged to form mental pictures of himself, like an actor on a screen, and see himself enjoying life in every way, laughing and joking with friends, going to cinemas, theatres and dances, and doing all the things a young man in his position would expect to do.

After six sessions Mr. —— stated that he felt he had overcome his old bogy for good. Three years later he wrote to say that he was now happily married and had had no return of his old 'ancestral jimjams,' as he called them. In fact he had taken the trouble to revisit his old home and had solemnly stared each disapproving ancestor full in the eyes while making a popular but nevertheless very rude gesture!

Chapter Twenty-eight

OBSESSIONAL NEUROSIS

Mrs. —— had a curious obsession. She couldn't stop eating. This in spite of the fact that she was grossly overweight and hated herself for being so ungainly and forced to wear unbecoming outsize clothes.

She stated that she longed to be slim so that she could wear attractive clothes and live a normal social life instead of being, as she thought, a 'figure of fun.'

No matter how she tried, she could never keep to a diet. As soon as she tried, she would become irritable and unhappy to an extraordinary degree.

It was not as though she enjoyed her food, for poor Mrs. —— stated she loathed the very idea of eating sweets and cakes, yet she felt compelled to do so almost against her will.

Her doctor stated that there was no glandular or organic disorder to account for her obesity, and in view of her feeling compelled to eat it seemed obvious that there was some deep psychological reason for her unfortunate condition.

As she told her life story it certainly seemed as though she had run up against a series of unfortunate circumstances. At the age of about five or six she had lost both her parents, who were killed in an accident. She remembered being brought up by grandparents, who had done all they could to make her happy. The next upset in her life was when she fell in love with her foreign music-teacher at about the age of sixteen. He was promptly sent away by the grandparents, and she remembered being very miserable and unhappy. Later she married, and although she made what was considered a 'good match' she was never really in love with her husband. She wanted to have children, but when none arrived they decided to adopt one. Unfortunately he had turned out to be a great disappointment, and after getting into trouble with the police had finally run away and was never heard of again.

Mrs. —— seemed to lose all interest in life after this, and found herself eating more and more and getting steadily fatter and fatter. The more weight she put on, the less inclined she felt to go out, and, as her social contacts became less and less, she felt more and more unhappy and miserable. Finally it seemed as though eating was the only interest she had in life, and she even loathed that. She could not understand why she should feel so compelled to eat sweet things.

She was told that there was a reason all right, and that, although she could not see it now, she would remember it during the course of treatment.

Accordingly, after she had learned to relax by hypnosis, Mrs. —— was given the suggestion that she would 'have a thought come into her head some time in the near future' and that this thought would tell her just why she went on craving sweets, which she knew were bad for her.

A week later Mrs. —— reported that it had all come back to her very clearly. She remembered quite easily and in great detail how frightened and upset she had been when her parents were killed. She had cried and cried and felt terribly miserable and unhappy. Her grandparents had been at their wit's end to know how to comfort her. She remembered her old grandfather taking her on his knee and nursing her for hours at a time. As he stroked her hair and told her stories to comfort her, he would keep giving her sweets, of which apparently he was very fond himself. The grandmother too would do the same, and Mrs. —— remembered how she felt happy only when being petted and fussed over and fed with sweets.

Now that she came to think of it, Mrs. —— remembered that when her first love affair had been broken up she had attempted to console herself by eating boxes of sweets! In fact, on thinking carefully over the events of her life, it seemed that every time something happened to make her feel unhappy she instinctively turned to sweets.

Of course it was quite obvious now even to Mrs. —— what had originally happened. As a little girl her mind had been emotionally upset by the loss of her parents. Her mind became concentrated on the idea that she felt happy only when being petted and fed with sweets, and this went on acting all her life with the force of hypnotic suggestion. Starved of affection by various circumstances, she felt forced to eat as much sweet food as she could.

Once she had realised the cause of her condition it was fairly easy to frame suggestions that would remove Mrs. ——'s obsession. Under hypnosis it was pointed out to her that she was no longer an unhappy little girl of five or six who had to be fed with sweets. Therefore she could give up that little girl's feelings. In future she would find it easy to keep to a diet, and as she lost weight she would be able to wear better clothes, mix with people again, and enjoy a reasonable life in a normal way. She was encouraged to form pictures in her mind, seeing herself attractively slim, and told that every time she kept to the diet she would have such pleasant pictures in her mind. Her doctor then gave her a carefully planned diet, and Mrs. —— had no difficulty in keeping to it after a few hypnotic sessions had convinced her she would be happier doing this than eating sweets. A year later Mrs. —— wrote to say that she had lost three stones in weight and felt as though she had been granted a new lease of life.

Chapter Twenty-nine

DEPRESSION

Mr. ——, a middle-aged married man, was the picture of misery when he came along.

His doctor's report described him as a case of depression. Mr. —— complained that he felt life was not worth living. Everything he attempted seemed to go wrong, and he had lost all confidence in himself. He seemed to have no powers of concentration left, and described his memory as 'shocking.' Apparently he suffered from frequent headaches, and slept very badly unless he took heavy doses of sleeping tablets.

Mr. —— was at a loss to explain the cause of his condition, but said he seemed to have gone steadily downhill after the age of about twenty-five. The change, he felt, was all the more remarkable as when he was a young man he was full of confidence.

As he proceeded to answer detailed questions designed to bring out any significant events in his past life, it seemed that as a young man Mr. —— had indeed been full of promise. He had done particularly well at school, especially at sports, and having won the school championship rather fancied himself as a boxer. Indeed, he had kept up his boxing after leaving school and managed to win one or two cups in amateur contests.

He had done well at work and had got on socially, but after about twenty-five he began to notice he was avoiding people more and more, as he felt uneasy in their company. This he could not understand, as he said he had always been a good mixer.

Shortly after this he began to suffer from headaches and sleep badly. As his condition became progressively worse, in spite of 'nerve tonics' and 'sleeping tablets,' he noticed that he was having frequent fits of deep depression when life seemed hardly worth living. This was in spite of the fact that he was quite happily married, had a good job, and on the face of it appeared to have everything to live for. Try as he would, he could not remember any domestic or business worry which could have started his trouble.

He was told, therefore, that he could give up striving and straining to remember. The thought of what had caused his trouble would come back to him easily enough later on, when he had learned to relax and calm his brain under hypnosis.

After he had practised his relaxing for a week, at the next hypnotic session he was given the suggestion that a thought would come into his head of its own accord, without any trying on his part, and that this thought would show him quite clearly what had started his trouble.

When he reported a week later Mr. —— said: 'I had a thought all right, and I'm sure it's what upset me.'

Thereupon he related the following story.

Apparently, one evening, in a fairly rough quarter of the town in which he lived, he had seen a man hitting his wife. The patient had immediately gone to her rescue and remonstrated with the man. The husband had been a very tough, ugly-looking customer indeed, and had promptly challenged our hero to a fight. To this day, the patient said, he could not understand what had happened. When he went over to interfere he had felt full of confidence, particularly in view of his boxing record. However, when challenged by this tough character, all his courage seemed to ooze out of him. He had turned on his heel and walked away, to the derisive shouts and jeers of a few onlookers. Burning with shame he had gone home feeling that he was a coward.

It was obvious now, even to Mr. ——, what had caused his trouble. At an emotional time, when his mind had been concentrated into a condition resembling hypnosis, the idea had been burned into his brain that he was a coward and could not face up to things in an emergency. The idea that he could really be a coward conflicted so much with his desires and previous opinion of himself that it set up terrific nervous tension.

As a result he began to suffer from headaches and insomnia. Worry and anxiety over these, and the idea of being a coward, created a vicious circle of thinking. As his mind became more and more occupied with his unpleasant feelings, naturally he was able to concentrate less and less. Taking a no real notice or interest in things meant that he could not remember them, and because of this he became afraid of his failing memory. In the beginning he had avoided people because he thought they might see he was a coward. As his symptoms became increasingly complex, he forgot more and more about the original 'cowardly' incident, and became aware only that he felt uncomfortable with people and wanted to avoid them. The original cause being gradually forgotten in his preoccupation with his unpleasant feelings, he began to feel that his mind must be going, as there did not seem anything else to account for his condition.

Naturally enough, a thought like this, on top of his other symptoms, was enough to depress anybody, hence his attacks of deep depression.

Once the patient had realised all this, it was relatively easy to persuade him by means of light hypnosis and suggestion to adopt a somewhat more adult attitude to his troubles. For instance, it was pointed out that he was no longer an emotionally upset young man of twenty-five, and he could give up feeling like one. In any case, he had done the only sensible thing in refusing a street brawl. Even a trained professional boxer would have probably done the same. It had taken courage to stop the man hitting his wife at all—many people would have looked the other way. Now things were different. He would be able to face up to the ordinary conditions of life in a normal way. With these and similar constructive suggestions it was soon possible to rebuild the patient's confidence and self-respect, and after a few weeks of treatment he stated that 'he felt a new man' and his depression was a thing of the past.

Chapter Thirty

ASTHMA

MRS. —— HAD suffered badly from asthma practically all her life. As she wheezed her way painfully through her story, with an occasional pause to take a puff from her portable inhaler, it became obvious that no stone had been left unturned in her effort to find some alleviation or cure for her distressing condition.

Although she could hardly remember a time when she did not suffer from asthma, there was one particular occasion which seemed to be impressed on her mind. She remembered going shopping with her mother as a little girl of about five or six. They were in a crowded lift when suddenly she felt she could not breathe and had a terrible feeling of panic. She remembered gasping for breath and creating such a scene that her mother had at first given her a smacking. Then becoming alarmed, as this, far from doing her good, only made her worse, she had rushed her to the doctor, who had promptly labelled her asthmatic.

After this the patient remembered she began to have attacks more and more frequently. At first they would come on only if she were in a confined space, such as a lift or a railway carriage or a small, closed room. As she became more and more afraid of the attacks, however, they started to come on at any time, until now she expected to have an attack at any moment.

All sorts of treatment had been tried. As a child her tonsils and adenoids had been removed, and later on her sinuses and antra had been drained. Teeth had been removed, and the most extensive investigations made into practically every organ and gland of the body in an effort to find some septic focus or other cause for her unfortunate condition. When these failed she had been tested to see if she were sensitive to various substances such as house dust, feathers or various pollens, but nothing definite was ever found. As a result poor Mrs. —— had to rely upon her inhaler to give her a little relief, and calling the doctor to give her an injection when she had a very bad attack.

When she had finished her story there did not seem to be anything outstanding to account for her condition. It seemed difficult to believe that the incident in the lift had caused her trouble, because she had been in lifts before this without any difficulty.

However, it was explained to Mrs. —— that asthma was only due to spasm of the bronchioles, and the spasm could come only as a result of a nervous message. And any nervous message which caused spasm or tension could come only from a frightening idea. Now she was afraid of her asthma, and it was only the fear of her asthma which was keeping it going. Something, somewhere, had been responsible for first frightening her and upsetting her breathing. Although her mind was too upset and preoccupied with her asthma at present for her to remember her original trouble, Mrs. —— was assured that she would be able to realise this quite clearly later on when her mind was calmer.

Accordingly, Mrs. —— was first taught how to relax under hypnosis. After a week of practice the patient already felt much more confident. Already she had begun to realise that all her drugs, inhalations and injections could do was to relax the bronchial muscles, and that if she could learn to relax naturally she would have no need of these artificial aids. Furthermore, if she could relax first by thinking about it, obviously she would be able to get relief by this method far more quickly than she could·hope to do by drugs.

Mrs. —— still had no idea, however, what could have first upset her, so during the second hypnotic session it was suggested that an idea would come into her mind some time in the near future. This thought, it was explained, would come without any trying on her part, probably when she least expected it, and it would show her quite clearly what had first frightened her and disturbed her breathing.

A week later the patient was all smiles when she came along for the third treatment. She had remembered a very remarkable incident.

Apparently she had two elder brothers who were generally regarded as 'little devils.' On one occasion when she had annoyed them by insisting on joining in some game or other they had locked her in a big old trunk. The patient had been terrified that she would suffocate, and her state of mind had not been improved by hearing her brothers dancing around and proclaiming loudly that she would die in the trunk, nobody would ever find her and she would turn into 'a nasty little skeleton'! As a matter of fact that patient had nearly been suffocated, for when her brothers opened the trunk again she had been unconscious.

Now it was obvious why she had had that attack in the lift. As a child crowded in with a lot of people in a closed space, it had reminded her of the terrible experience in the trunk. This being associated with the idea of suffocation had naturally upset her breathing and caused her first attack of asthma. As she became more and more afraid of her attacks, she had gradually forgotten the original cause of her trouble. As she realised the hidden cause of her fears, it proved fairly easy to persuade Mrs. ——, under light hypnosis, that as she was no longer a frightened little girl she could give up having a frightened little girl's feelings. Therefore she could relax and always breathe freely and easily in the future. In fact she could give up worrying about how she breathed at all, and just let everything work naturally and normally. Within a few weeks Mrs. —— was able to report that her 'asthma' had gone and she felt as though she had 'a new lease of life.'

Chapter Thirty-one

INSOMNIA

Mrs. ——, a middle-aged widow, complained of severe insomnia for many years. She had the greatest difficulty in getting off to sleep, and if she did manage it with the aid of heavy doses of sleeping drugs she would invariably wake up with a feeling of panic in the early hours of the morning. She attributed her trouble to worry and grief following the death of her husband, but as she told her story it soon became obvious that there was a much deeper and more fundamental cause. To begin with, it appeared she had suffered from insomnia before her husband died or had even been ill. Further, it appeared that her insomnia only troubled her when she had to sleep alone. According to her story she used to make a habit as a child of leaving her own bed and sleeping with her sister. When the sister, who was older, went to boarding school and the patient was left alone she began to sleep very badly and dreaded the approach of bedtime. When she got married she was able to sleep with her husband, but when left alone after his death her insomnia reappeared.

It appeared obvious from her story that being alone somehow meant danger, and in time of danger Nature has arranged that a person does not go to sleep.

Mrs. —— was quite unable to think why she should have always disliked sleeping alone. It was explained to her that now it was her fear of insomnia which was keeping her awake, for the nervous system is unable to tell the difference between one fear and another. The response to fear of any kind is always the same—'get ready to fight or run away'—and in either case a person does not settle down to sleep! Although it was her fear of insomnia now which kept her awake something, somewhere, some time had given her the idea that there was 'danger' in going to sleep on her own.

Mrs. —— was told not to strain herself trying to remember what it was that had first frightened her. The thought would come into her head on its own account—just as a forgotten telephone number or name will often come back to mind without trying—when she learned to relax and her mind could work more and more calmly.

Accordingly, Mrs. —— was given instructions how to relax under hypnosis and how to practise it for herself. At a later session the suggestion was given that some time in the near future a thought would come into her mind without trying and that this would show her quite clearly what had first frightened her, although it would be unable to frighten her now.

When she came along for the third session Mrs. —— was very excited, for she had remembered what had upset her, and related the following remarkable story.

Apparently as a little girl she had heard her parents talking about somebody and say: 'Of course, she must have a skeleton in the cupboard.'

The patient had wondered what it meant, and had asked her sister if they had a skeleton in the cupboard, not knowing, of course, what the phrase implied. Her sister, to frighten her, had said: 'Oh yes, we've got one. It lives in the bedroom cupboard and comes out at night when you're asleep. If you ask too many questions it will come out and get you.'

A few nights later the patient had a nightmare and dreamed that a fearful skeleton was coming to 'get' her. She wakened screaming with fear and imagined she could see the skeleton. To quieten her the sister allowed her to sleep in her bed, and ever after the patient would always sleep with her sister.

It became very obvious even to Mrs. —— why she feared sleeping alone. Long ago, as a child, her mind had been concentrated by an emotional circumstance into a condition of hypnosis, for all practical purposes. In this state the idea that sleeping alone meant fear and danger had been implanted with the force of a hypnotic suggestion.

Now that she recognised the hitherto apparently mysterious cause of her insomnia Mrs. —— felt considerably relieved in her mind. However, as it was explained to her, simply knowing the cause would not cure her by itself. It did, however, indicate the lines on which the curative suggestions should be based. For instance, it was impressed on Mrs. —— during the hypnotic sessions that as she was no longer a frightened little girl she could give up feeling like one. Therefore she could sleep alone in perfect confidence. These and other constructive suggestions soon enabled Mrs. —— to report that she had given up her sleeping drugs, was now sleeping quite naturally and awakened feeling fit and refreshed each morning.

Chapter Thirty-two

MIGRAINE

'MR. ——,' HIS doctor wrote, 'suffers from frequent and severe attacks of migraine. He is thirty years of age and happily married, but his complaint seems to be ruining his domestic, social and business life. The attacks appear to have begun on leaving the Army after the war and setting up in civilian life. He is trying to study for accountancy, but his headaches seem to be spoiling his chances. He has been thoroughly investigated, but there does not seem to be any physical defect or organic disorder to account for his condition. Apart from an attack of malaria during his service abroad, he seems to have a completely clean bill of health. He is a conscientious sort and very keen to get on. I am inclined to think there must be some psychological upset which is either causing or aggravating his condition. He has had all the usual medical treatment, but, although an injection helps to cut short the actual attack, nothing seems to prevent their frequent occurrence—usually at the most inopportune time.'

As Mr. —— related his symptoms, it was quite obvious that his doctor's diagnosis was quite correct. First of all, he said, he felt such a fool. He had always been 'as strong as a horse' and had prided himself on his 'terrific will-power.' Women and girls he had always believed were the only ones who got the 'megrims' or 'vapours.' Although a few attacks had convinced him that he could not fight against them, he still fretted and fumed at being what he called a 'sissy.'

The trouble was, he said, that he could never be sure of keeping appointments, and never knew if he would be able to go to a cinema or theatre. More than likely, if his wife wanted to go out to a dance or to enjoy a special evening with friends, he would spoil it all by having a migraine attack. Apparently it was becoming a bit of a joke, although a source of acute embarrassment to his wife and himself, for several of his unthinking friends would tease him by inquiring if he'd had the 'vapours' again.

The patient stated that he found it practically impossible to study, and he had such difficulty in concentrating on his work that he half expected to 'get the sack' at any time.

From his description it was very clear that Mr. —— suffered from genuine migraine. First of all he would notice a blurring of the vision of one eye, usually the right. Then he would get 'flashes of light' and the headache would begin. This would take the form of a boring pain in the eyeball which would gradually get worse and spread all over one side of the head. The headaches were so bad that the patient would have to lie down, and any noise, movement or bright light would make it worse. Finally he would feel sick and vomit, and after this the headache would gradually pass off.

The whole attack would last for about a day, he said, and he never felt quite normal for two or three days afterwards. During the attacks he often wished he could die, and described the feeling as being 'about a hundred times worse than sea-sickness.'

Well, when Mr. —— had finished his tale of woe, it was possible to give him a grain of comfort as a sop to his self-esteem. Plenty of men, he was informed, were martyrs to migraine. In this way it was just like seasickness, which was notoriously no respecter of persons. Many men much tougher than he was had been laid low by seasickness, and even some Commandos were knocked out by it. Even the great Nelson had been seasick every time he went to sea, so he could give up fretting and fuming about being a 'sissy.' Further, he could pride himself on one thing, for it was the highly intelligent, intellectual type of person who suffered most from migraine.

Now, in going through his history there did not seem anything to indicate why he should have developed this condition. His marriage had been quite happy, although he felt that his wife must be feeling the strain of his illness.

He was told, therefore, that now it was only the worry over his condition which was keeping it going, and that as soon as he learned to relax and stop worrying about it, the condition would disappear. Something, however, had started the worry, and by causing tension in the head had given rise to his attacks. What this was he would be able to remember later on when he had learned to relax and his brain could think more calmly.

Accordingly, after he had learned to relax under hypnosis and practised for a week himself, the suggestion was given during the next session that he would realise quite clearly without effort what it was that had first worried him.

Sure enough when he reported for treatment again he had the following story to tell. Apparently, having left the Army after an exciting war service, and being newly married, Mr. —— had found it very difficult to settle down to civilian life. Being ambitious, he knew that he would have to work hard to get on, but his job in a firm of accountants seemed incredibly boring after his life on active service. It was obvious that he would have to study hard to pass his examinations in accountancy. At the same time, he could see that his wife wanted to go out, entertain and enjoy a bright social life, and indeed he felt much the same himself. However, when they went out to enjoy themselves he would find himself thinking that he was wasting time, and that he should be studying so that he would get on in the world. On the other hand, when he tried to settle down to study, he kept thinking how boring it was, how his wife must be hating to miss parties and dances. As a result poor Mr. —— felt his mind being pulled in two directions, so it was no wonder that he soon began to develop headaches. Worry over these merely aggravated his condition and soon produced a typical attack of migraine. Once he had experienced this, fear of the condition created sufficient tension to keep it going. As he became more and more preoccupied with his unpleasant symptoms, he had soon forgotten the original cause of his trouble.

When he realised all this in his calmer frame of mind, Mr. —— could see where he had gone wrong. It did not need many more sessions of hypnosis to convince him that it was not a case of all work or all play. Now and in future it was suggested he would be able to portion out his time. 'All work and no play makes Jack a dull boy,' so he would be able to concentrate his mind on his work when he was at work and let nothing distract him but when he went out to enjoy himself with his wife no thoughts of work or study would interfere with his pleasure.

It was a very pleased Mr. —— who was soon able to report that his 'vapours' and 'megrims' were things of the past, and that he was now able to work, study and enjoy life in a perfectly normal way.

Chapter Thirty-three

ALCOHOLISM

MR. —— WAS a promising lawyer—or rather he had been until he started drinking too much and appeared to pay more attention to the bar of the public house than the Bar of the Law Court.

When seen, he stated that he felt he could not go on much longer. Apparently he did legal work for some local authority, and he felt sure that his condition had not passed altogether unnoticed on several occasions. Actually, he said, he hated drink, but felt he had to take it to 'steady his nerves.'

It seemed that he was always nervous in the Court, and had an abnormal fear that things would go wrong. As a result he was always worrying about the cases and papers he had to prepare, so that he would go over things again and again to 'make sure.'

All this worry and anxiety naturally upset him, and he suffered from nervous indigestion, felt tired and exhausted and often depressed at what he regarded as a very black outlook in life. His memory and concentration had suffered a good deal, and it seemed to him, so he said, that he did not want to think.

He felt dreadfully inferior and ashamed of himself, and seemed to be abnormally afraid of offending people. In Court he would quake inwardly, and said that he was sure he was always more afraid than the person against whom he was appearing!

There did not seem to be any particular reason why he should be so nervous and take to drink. He had gone through the war without any particular sign of nerves, and while he had certainly learned to drink during this time, it had not been to excess. He was happily married and had no anxieties on this score, although his wife was naturally beginning to feel the strain of his excessive drinking.

He seemed to date the onset of his nervousness from one particular case in Court. Everything had been going well when suddenly, as one witness was giving evidence, he started to 'shake inside.' He had such an attack of panic that he thought he was going to faint. There did not seem to be any particular reason for his panic, but he was so upset that he made a complete mess of his case and lost it. He had an idea that everybody could see there was something wrong. Ever after he began to feel panicky at the idea of going to Court, and soon began to take a nip of something to steady his nerves. Gradually he found that his 'nerves' were coming on at other times outside the Court, so he began to drink more and more frequently to give himself confidence or Dutch courage. When he noticed how much he was drinking, he became alarmed at the prospect of becoming a confirmed alcoholic. This idea frightened him all the more, so that he developed more 'nerves' and needed more drink.

When poor Mr. —— had finished his sorry tale he was given a grain of comfort. It was explained that really alcoholics were only people who suffered from nervous tension and had to take alcohol simply because they knew of no other way to overcome their nervous tension. He would be able to give up alcohol quite easily, he was told, when he had learned to relax naturally. Now it was the fear of alcoholism which was manufacturing the nervous tension and so keeping his unfortunate condition going. Something, however, had caused his first attack of panic and given rise to those unpleasant feelings which made him turn to alcohol for relief.

Although he could not remember what it was *now*, owing to the flustered state of his mind, he would see it all quite clearly when he had learned to relax and his mind became calmer.

Accordingly, Mr. —— started on a course of hypnotic treatment, and was first of all taught how to relax. After a week's practice he reported that he already felt a lot steadier, although, of course, he was by no means cured.

During the second hypnotic session he was given the suggestion that he would remember quite well what it was that upset him. When he came along for the third treatment, Mr. —— said: 'Well, I know what it was all right, and it's so damn silly I feel ashamed to tell you.'

Apparently he had been brought up in the Midlands. When he went to his public school he suffered a great deal of ragging on account of his accent. One master in particular used to 'take it out of him.' He would often have him out in front of the class and make him recite or read out passages which revealed only too painfully his Midland accent. Of course, the others in the class would laugh and he was teased unmercifully afterwards.

The patient said that even now he could remember how he felt he would die of shame, and had often wished he could sink out of sight through the floor. The teacher he hated most would always finish up a session of teasing by saying: 'You'd better get rid of that dreadful accent or you'll never go anywhere in life.'

Well, in the years that followed poor Mr. —— made superhuman efforts to lose the accent, and by the time he had qualified regarded himself, as he said, as practically B.B.C.!

Now comes the extraordinary part of his story. The witness he was questioning in Court came from the same part of the country as the patient. He spoke with the dreadful accent, and in the heat of the exchanges the patient remembered that he had forgotten his B.B.C. accent and let fall a word in the local dialect.

Immediately all the old fears which he thought he had forgotten came crowding back. He thought everybody was laughing at him. He could hardly see the Court. In fact, in his mind he was a boy back at school, making a fool of himself in front of the whole class. In his panic he had made a mess of things, hardly knowing what he was doing.

Yes, as Mr. —— had said, it was a damn silly thing, but it had started him on the downhill path.

Once he had realised all this and got it out of his system, Mr. —— felt better. A few hypnotic sessions were sufficient to convince him that he was no longer a little boy being made fun of in front of the class, and so he could give up having this little boy's feelings. In future he would be able to stand up for himself in Court or anywhere else and feel perfectly confident. As for his accent, he would not care two hoots about it. He was encouraged to form 'success pictures' in his mind and see himself as he wanted to be—calm, confident and successful.

A few weeks later Mr. —— was able to report that he was indeed a new man, and, as he felt no need for alcohol, had given it up altogether.

Chapter Thirty-four

EXCESSIVE SMOKING

LITTLE MR. —— was obviously feeling the effects of his excessive smoking. Sixty cigarettes a day, besides costing him much more than he could afford, were giving him headaches, attacks of giddiness, palpitation and nervous indigestion. He slept badly, had no real appetite and felt nervous and irritable.

His memory, he said, was getting worse every day, and he did not seem able to concentrate on anything. Apparently he had been smoking ever since he was a boy, but had realised during the last few years that he was now doing so to excess. He had made one or two half-hearted efforts to give it up, but he had never managed to go without a cigarette for more than a day or so. And then, he said, he felt much worse than when he smoked! Now, however, he felt that the time had come for him to be forced to give up smoking by hypnotism.

It was explained to Mr. —— that this was not the way to cure smoking. There was a definite reason for his excessive craving for tobacco. Even if he could be forced to give up tobacco against his desires, something worse would take its place— perhaps a craving for drugs or alcohol—unless the cause of his trouble was discovered and treated.

Mr. —— could not think why he should be so addicted to 'the weed,' but it was pointed out to him that his trouble followed a familiar pattern. Now he was worried about his excessive smoking and the ill effects on his health. This worry merely created more nervous tension, and the only thing he knew which would relieve this tension was a cigarette in oft-repeated doses. Therefore he was caught up in a vicious circle. However, something had started him feeling nervous and given him the idea that a cigarette was the answer to his problem.

Try as he would, however, Mr. —— could not remember

anything very significant. It seemed to him that he had always smoked, even as a schoolboy!

He was told, therefore, to give up striving to remember, as he would think about what it was quite automatically after he had learnt to relax. Hypnotic treatment was therefore started, and directed towards teaching him how to relax naturally and calm his nerves. Even at the end of the first week Mr. —— said he felt calmer and had been able to reduce his cigarettes by a few each day. However, it was explained that this slight improvement was due only to his increased ability to relax, and that the real cure was yet to come.

During the second session it was suggested that he would remember very clearly what had first made him nervous and put the idea of cigarettes into his head.

When the patient came along for the third session he had an extraordinary story to relate. Apparently as a child he had been very thin and weak and rather inclined to a humped back. Even now he was only a little man, below average size and rather of the weedy type. As a child, therefore, he was rather pushed about by the others, and this was aggravated by the fact that his parents moved about a great deal and he had gone to no less than ten different schools. It seemed that he was always the 'new boy.' At a very early age he had copied his father smoking and found that this greatly increased his prestige at school! Therefore he made a habit of showing off by smoking in front of the others. This trick was particularly useful when he had to face a new school. Although he was weak and puny he could literally 'smoke the bigger boys under the table.'

As he grew up he found himself smoking more and more. It seemed that he would have to smoke before facing any important task, particularly one which involved meeting people. As Mr. —— was a traveller, he soon found himself literally chain-smoking. He would smoke while driving the car, often stop a short way from the customer's place of business and smoke a cigarette before going in to see the man, and then, of course, smoke with him if possible. Poor Mr. —— could hardly imagine the idea of approaching a customer, or indeed anybody, 'in cold blood' without a cigarette to bolster up his courage.

When he realised this Mr. —— could see how silly it all was. However, it remained for him to 'feel' that he could face up to life without cigarettes. Therefore several hypnotic sessions were devoted to building up his morale and self-esteem. It was pointed out to him that he was no longer a weak little boy, so he did not need to keep a weak little boy's nervous feelings. Now he was a grown-up business man who could face people and feel perfectly confident and at ease without cigarettes. He was encouraged to see himself as he wished to be by forming imaginary pictures in his mind. Thus he conjured up little 'success' pictures, seeing himself full of confidence talking business to a customer without smoking. These and other similar constructive suggestions soon enabled Mr. —— to report that he had been able to give up smoking completely, and felt all the better for it in every way.

Chapter Thirty-five

STAMMERING

'I SHOULD BE glad if something can be done for Mr.——'s stammer,' wrote his doctor. 'He is a nice young fellow, but his handicap seems to be ruining his life. Embarrassment makes him avoid social contacts and is holding him back from getting on at work.'

As poor Mr. —— tried to tell his story, it was obvious how handicapped he was. There he was struggling and straining, but the words just would not seem to come out.

He was told to give up straining and try whispering. Practically all stammerers can talk perfectly well if they whisper. As will be seen later, stammering is only due to tension and when the victims give up straining they can nearly always do very well. Anyway, Mr. —— managed to answer all the questions and gradually a picture of his life was built up. It followed fairly closely the usual pattern. Apparently, it seemed to him, he had stammered all his life. He could not remember any particular incident which might have started his condition, but he could remember plenty which had made his life a misery!

At school, for instance, he had had a very bad time. Various masters had made a fool of him and he suffered a great deal of ragging and teasing from the others. Reading in class was a nightmare. Later, when he left school, he did his best to avoid people on account of his handicap. Shopping caused him a great deal of embarrassment, as he felt everybody was looking at him as he struggled to get out what he wanted to say. He hated the idea of travelling on a bus or train and asking for a ticket. At work he was hopeless on the telephone and the butt of the office 'wits.' With the boss he was practically speechless, as he was always worse with anybody in authority.

Strangely enough, Mr. —— could speak perfectly well to his pet dog if there were nobody there, and he could talk or read to himself without difficulty. He was at a loss to understand this, for it seemed odd that his speech should be quite free and easy at one moment and then practically hopeless the next.

However, it was explained to Mr. —— that this was quite usual with stammerers. The reason he could speak perfectly well to a dog when alone was that he knew the dog couldn't criticise him. Therefore there was no fear of making a mistake when speaking to his dog. This provided a pointer to the real cause of his condition. With people he was afraid of making a mistake in his speech. Therefore when he came to speak to *people*—either in person or on the telephone—he automatically *tensed* himself to make a great effort. It was this tension which interfered with the muscles of speech, his vocal cords and breathing apparatus and so produced the stammer. In fact, the harder he tried the worse he did, which was why when he gave up straining and simply whispered he did much better.

He was told that he would have to learn to care no more about speaking to people than he did with his dog if he wanted to be cured.

Now it was only the fear of making a fool of himself in front of people which kept his stammer going. However, something in the past had first frightened him and given him the idea that speaking to people could be dangerous, especially if he made a mistake.

Mr. —— was quite mystified and said that he could not remember anything like that as a child.

It was suggested that he should give up worrying about it, as the memory of anything important would come back quite easily once he had learned to relax and take things rather more calmly.

Accordingly Mr. —— was started on a course of hypnotic treatment designed in the first place to teach him how to relax instead of tightening himself up whenever he came to speak.

At the second session it was suggested that he would have a thought come into his head which would show him quite clearly what had first frightened him.

When he came along for the third treatment he had the following remarkable story to relate. He remembered that when a child he had lived next door to a family who had a rather half-witted boy. This poor boy drooled and made very odd noises when he spoke, or rather tried to say something, for he could hardly say a word properly. One day the patient, when about four or five, had been imitating him. His father, who happened to hear him, had been furiously angry. Probably he did not like his son making fun of the poor half-wit, or he may have been afraid that the boy would copy him. In any case he had lost his temper and stormed at the patient, saying 'I'll burn your tongue out if I ever hear you speaking badly again.' And so saying, no doubt to impress the patient, he had grabbed him by the arm and barely touched it with the lighted end of his cigarette.

'There,' he had said, 'you'll feel it a lot more on the tongue if I hear of any more of your nonsense.' Although his skin had not been actually burnt, the patient was terrified and practically 'screamed his head off.' Every time he had to speak in the presence of his father he had a constant dread of making a mistake and having his tongue burnt.

Soon the tension interfered with his speech, and although his father never carried out his foolish threat nevertheless the patient said he gradually got to the stage where he was practically speechless in the presence of his father. Soon the condition developed until anybody who even reminded him of his father —a school-teacher for instance—would upset his speech. The ragging in school did the rest, until the patient gradually became convinced that he would have difficulty in speaking to anybody.

At an emotional time his mind had been concentrated and the idea fixed in his brain with the force of a hypnotic suggestion.

Treatment was therefore directed to convincing Mr. —— that he was no longer a frightened little boy and so he no longer needed the little boy's feelings. Nobody was going to burn his tongue now if he made a mistake. In fact probably nobody cared at all whether he stammered or not. He would therefore give up worrying also, relax and feel at ease when he spoke to people the same as he did with his dog.

As a result of these and similar constructive suggestions, such as forming mental pictures and 'seeing' himself speaking with confidence under conditions he knew he would have to face, Mr. —— was soon able to report, after a few weeks' treatment, that he could now speak to people with confidence.

Chapter Thirty-six

BLUSHING

'I FEEL SUCH a fool,' said Mr. —— when he came along for consultation. 'Here I am, a middle-aged business man, and I blush like a silly schoolgirl.'

As his story unfolded it was impossible not to feel sorry for him. In common with all people who blush, he suffered agonies of embarrassment. Apparently he would go 'scarlet' on the slightest provocation, especially if it seemed that attention was being drawn to him in any way.

He was married, but his social life appeared to be practically nil. Naturally enough his wife resented the fact that they could never go out to friends or entertain them at home. At work Mr. —— suffered agonies, particularly as he thought the girls in the office all knew about his habit and giggled at him behind his back. This silly habit, he said, had led to a feeling of acute inferiority and he felt he would have done much better in business but for this unfortunate handicap.

When asked exactly why he feared blushing so much, he said: 'Oh, it makes me feel such a fool in front of people. I feel they can see I'm nervous and inferior.' When it is analysed, all people who blush seem to feel like this. They feel as if the dreaded red flush were a huge placard hanging around their neck announcing to all the world in big bold letters 'I'm nervous —I'm inferior' or some other equally dispiriting statement. Therefore they come to hate and fear the habit of blushing because they regard it as a tell-tale sign of their inferiority. It is bad enough to feel inferior, but to have the fact blazoned abroad is too much, they feel.

It was pointed out to Mr. —— that it was only because he hated and feared his blushing that he kept the habit going. Practically everybody blushes at some time or other, particularly in youth when the nervous system is not so stable. Most people, however, do not worry about it and, therefore, as the nervous system becomes more stable they are never troubled by it.

A blush only means that the blood vessels of the face and neck are dilated to let in more blood. These blood vessels, as indeed are others in the body, are surrounded by a network of nerves so that they dilate or contract in response to messages received from the brain. Practically everybody has heard of a little animal called a chameleon whose idea of protection is to change colour to camouflage itself. Blushing is a sort of primitive defence mechanism in an effort to hide under conditions of shame, humiliation or possible danger.

Now, Mr.——was told, the fear of blushing was the very thing which was constantly manufacturing nervous tension. This, by upsetting the balance of his nervous system, was the only thing which kept his unfortunate habit going. He would be cured only when he gave up fearing he would blush. Although it was merely his own fear which was keeping the habit going, somewhere in the past he had been shamed and humiliated in such a fashion that his nervous system had never forgotten it. Mr.——, however, beyond volunteering the information that it seemed to him that he had always blushed, could think of no likely incident. It was explained to him that no doubt he would remember it quite easily once he had learned to relax, and so he started on a course of hypnotic treatment.

As with the other cases, a thought did come into his head in response to suggestion under hypnosis.

Apparently at about the age of five or six he had been at a children's party. As usual the mothers had been discussing the children, and during a sudden pause in the general hum of conversation the patient heard one well-meaning mother say, while pointing to him: 'What lovely fair curls—he ought to be a little girl.' At that age, to be mistaken for a girl was the greatest insult that could be offered! The patient had felt furious and gone scarlet with shame and humiliation. At this, to make matters worse, the silly woman had said : 'Oh, look, I do believe he's blushing.'

Several of the other children had noticed it and teased him both at the party and later on. All through his school life he had to put up with all sorts of humiliating taunts such as 'Look at old so-and-so, he's blushing like a girl.'

The patient had literally been self-hypnotised into blushing. At the time of the emotional incident at the children's party his mind had been concentrated into a state akin to hypnosis. The idea had been implanted with the force of a hypnotic suggestion that when attention was drawn to him he became an object of ridicule, while his shame and humiliation were made apparent to all in a tell-tale rush of blood to the face.

As he recalled all this Mr. —— felt considerably relieved, but it was explained that he would need several sessions to calm down his excitable nervous system.

Accordingly he was taught to relax and feel *at ease* with people—so much at ease that he would forget even to think about blushing. In addition he was encouraged to form 'success' pictures of himself behaving in the way he would like to act in circumstances he knew he would meet in everyday life. As a result it was not many weeks before he was able to report that he had lost his habit of blushing and now felt perfectly at ease with people. Some time later his wife wrote to say how pleased she was at the change in him and that it had made all the difference to their married and social life.

Chapter Thirty-seven

IMPOTENCE

Mr. ——, a middle-aged business man, was worried. So was his wife. Apparently they had been married just over two years, but the marriage was a marriage in name only.

'Mr. ——,' wrote his doctor, 'is quite normal organically. All the usual investigations have proved negative. It is my belief that his trouble is psychological.'

His doctor was right. Mr. —— did have something on his mind. Now, it was explained to him, he was afraid of his impotence and that it would lead to the break-up of his marriage. When fear of any kind came into the picture the person concerned always got ready to 'fight or run away.'

In either 'fighting' or 'running away' Nature had arranged that a man, or woman for that matter as well, did not get sexual feelings.

If being chased by a tiger or a wild bull, for instance, even the most amorous and virile lover would pay scant attention to the object of his affections.

Wild bulls and tigers were not ordinarily encountered in our state of civilisation, but there were other things which could inspire almost as much fear.

Now his fear of failure and appearing ridiculous were the very things which were causing the trouble.

Some time in the past, however, the idea had got into his head that sex was somehow wrong or difficult or dangerous.

Mr. ——, however, could not remember anything outstanding as a child. Apparently he had been brought up to be very much a mother's boy. His mother, deserted by her husband, had always impressed upon him how he must respect his sisters and look up to her and women in general. He remembered how she used to talk of his father as a 'bad man who would come to no good, as he didn't respect women,' and say: 'I hope you will never be like him.'

His father had, apparently, run off with some other woman, and was generally held up to be a model of what a man should *not* be! Apart from being warned against 'bad women,' Mr. —— could not remember anything else significant, but he never felt at ease with women, and until his marriage late in middle age he had had little to do with them.

However, it was obvious that there must be something deeper, that Mr. —— had forgotten, in order to account for his unnatural condition.

He was advised therefore to give up trying to remember and start learning to relax, when it was practically certain something significant would come into his mind as he became calmer.

After he had learned to relax for himself the idea was introduced during a session of hypnosis that he would recall any incident which had really upset him and made him fear making advances to women.

A week later Mr. —— had the solution. One day, apparently, when he was about seven or eight his mother had found him playing with the little girl next door and taking her clothes off. It was only childish curiosity, of course, but his mother was horrified. She had given him a good hiding and a tongue-lashing as well. Evidently she had vented all her hatred for her erring husband on poor Mr. ——. He remembered being told he was just like his father and God would punish him for his wickedness, and so on. He was certain to go to Hell and be burned up for ever if he so much as dared to insult a girl again.

The patient remembered being terrified and quite certain that the heavens would fall on him at any minute. Even after this incident he had frequent reminders about how he must 'respect' women and 'never do anything wrong' or God would punish him. Later when news of his father's death arrived he was told: 'I knew God would punish him for his wicked ways with women.' Mr. —— remembered how if he ever felt faint stirrings of sexual feelings he was sure he would be struck dead too.

Well, when he had got all this off his chest, Mr. —— felt a lot better. He could see how he had been led to believe sex was wrong and therefore his wife had become a symbol of danger for him.

'Mum' had been present on his honeymoon—not in person but in his mind. No wonder he failed!

Several sessions of hypnosis were necessary before 'Mum' and her warnings could be dispelled from the patient's mind, but eventually Mr. —— was able to report complete success and stated that he felt he had been given a new lease of life.

Chapter Thirty-eight

FRIGIDITY

'MRS. —— HAS a curious obsession,' wrote her doctor, 'she is insanely jealous of her husband. She accuses him of looking at the pictures of 'pin-up girls' in the newspapers, and things have got to such a pitch that she won't have a newspaper or magazine in the house. The poor man is afraid to look anywhere lest he be accused of philandering. If something isn't done soon I am afraid the marriage is headed for the rocks.'

When Mrs. —— came along she confirmed this almost unbelievable story. It was silly, she said, but she could not help feeling jealous. Then, as if to justify herself, she added that she was sure her husband did look at the pictures of bathing girls and film actresses in the newspapers.

It was pointed out to Mrs. —— that the cinema, theatre, newspaper and magazine world all depended upon the fact that the sexes were interested in one another, and it was common enough for men to look at pictures of bathing beauties and other 'pin-up' types and no doubt many women admired their screen heroes.

Mrs. —— agreed, but pointed out that in her case it was different as her husband paid more attention to his 'pin-up' pictures than he did to her!

Now here was something that required explanation. No ordinary man is going to be satisfied with pictures instead of a real woman.

A few questions soon revealed the trouble. Mrs. —— said she was unable to have a natural married life with her husband. She would like to, she said, but unfortunately she just felt quite 'dead' where sex was concerned. It was not that she thought there was anything particularly wrong with it, but she just was not interested. She could not see why a marriage could not be happy and successful without sex.

Under these circumstances Mrs. —— was told she was lucky that her husband only looked at pictures instead of other women. If she did not change her ideas soon it would not be surprising if he began to take an interest in real women. It was obvious that there must be something which had stopped the development of her normal feelings. At that moment she felt jealous of these 'picture women,' and no doubt this was because she realised that she was inferior in not acting as a real woman. No real woman could feel jealous or inferior to a 'pin-up' picture. Therefore it was necessary to find out what had given her the idea that had caused her trouble.

The patient professed a complete ignorance of anything which could have influenced her in early life. Apparently the honeymoon had not been very successful, and she admitted that she did feel a bit inferior and thought that she wished she could be like other women.

Mrs. —— was told that it was no good straining to try to remember things now, as her mind was in a state of turmoil, but that she would think of some significant incident later on.

After the patient had learned to relax and had practised on her own for a week the suggestion was given that she would remember what first upset her.

Her story when she came along for the third session was remarkable.

Apparently, as a child of five or six she had lived with her grandmother. The old lady evidently had a big varicose ulcer on her leg and one day the little girl saw her dressing it. Evidently she had asked what caused it and the old grandmother had said: 'Oh, it's all your grandfather's fault. He makes me work too hard. All men are the same.'

Now, Mrs. —— said, she remembered thinking: 'I must be careful of men—they might hurt me.' Following this she got the idea that if she felt 'numb and dead' then nobody could hurt her. During an emotional time such as the honeymoon this old idea had come flooding back to her. She had literally hypnotised herself into feeling 'numb and dead.' Small wonder it was that she had no real feelings for her husband. This failure had made her feel inferior, and as her coldness drove her husband farther and farther away from her, both emotionally and physically, she began to develop her jealousy.

When Mrs. —— had realised all this she could see how foolish it was for her to go on acting like a frightened little girl.

Therefore several sessions were directed to building up her morale and suggesting that now she was no longer a little girl she would act and feel like a grown-up woman, and as a real wife would have no feelings of jealousy for mere photographs. Some weeks later Mrs. —— reported that the treatment had been successful and she now looked forward to a happy married life.

Chapter Thirty-nine

THE CASE OF THE COLONEL

EVERY YEAR THREE thousand people die of asthma. Yet asthma—except possibly for some very rare forms—is not a disease; it is a sign of nervous tension.

Abolish that nervous tension, and there just isn't any reason for the asthma to persist.

When hypnosis is used to reveal the root cause of the trouble, the desired result usually follows as a matter of course so long as the patient wants to get well.

Given this co-operation, the treatment is unlikely to fail; but the case of Colonel—— is worth quoting as the exception that proves the rule, as far as co-operation is concerned.

Dr. —— wrote to say that he had a patient, a married man of over sixty years of age, who suffered so badly from 'asthma' that he feared for his life. Apparently the patient spent hours and hours leaning over the side of the bed gasping for breath, coughing and bringing up vast quantities of frothy material, and could never manage to get out of bed until late in the afternoon. Many years of this complaint had reduced him to a mere skeleton of little more than seven stone, his normal weight having been well over twelve stone. Injections and drugs such as Ephedrine now caused such alarming attacks of palpitation owing to the patient's weakened and exhausted condition that the doctor feared to continue with them. The patient, said the doctor, was a very obstinate man who 'did not believe in hypnotism or any of that rubbish,' but he had agreed to see a hypnotist 'as a last resort,' ostensibly to please the doctor, although the real reason was probably because he was at last frightened of dying.

When he arrived for consultation he announced quite bluntly that he 'wasn't going to let anybody control his will' and promptly turned his back, steadfastly refusing to look at the hypnotist! He agreed, however, that there could not be much danger in discussing his case, and with many promptings proceeded to unfold the following remarkable story.

Apparently during the first world war he had conducted himself with such bravery and distinction that after it was over he had been asked to train the armed service of a foreign Power. This he had done, and had enjoyed a very distinguished career. When the second world war began he immediately offered his services, but had been turned down as 'too old.' Apparently this had been done in a particularly tactless fashion by a supercilious and much younger man, evidently ignorant of the distinguished career of the patient, and he had been dismissed with some such flippant remark as 'Run along, Grandad, we're not using bows and arrows now, you know!' The patient had gone home 'choking with suppressed rage and matters were not improved when his wife voiced her opinion that the young man was probably quite right and he was far too old to think about going to war anyway!

Within a few days the patient was having 'typical asthma attacks,' which, in spite of all the doctor's efforts, rapidly progressed to the stage where he spent most of the day in bed vainly trying to 'get something off his chest.'

It was pointed out to the patient that what he was really trying 'to get off his chest' was his resentment at having been turned down and his anger at the supercilious young man at the War Office. Bottling up his fury at the time had created nervous tension—this had expressed itself in his lungs. The resulting 'asthma' attacks had frightened him, created more tension and so led to the establishment of a vicious circle.

The patient appeared to be much relieved at this explanation and made as dignified an exit as possible under his self-made conditions which demanded that he should not look at the hypnotist! He agreed, however, that a little relaxation and concentrated suggestion might be advisable and promised to come back later for a course of treatment.

A few day afterwards, however, he wrote a most extraordinary letter. 'Since my visit to you,' he wrote, 'there has been such an amazing improvement that I feel I am cured and do not need any more treatment. In fact I felt so well the day after

I saw you that I got up and went for a walk—a thing I have not done for many years.'

Bearing in mind that the patient had a rooted fear of hypnotism, it was considered possible that he was only making up this story in order to escape treatment. His doctor was therefore asked to report upon his condition, and his reply confirmed the patient's story in every particular. 'I don't know what cured him,' he wrote, 'and I don't profess to understand how it happened, but as long as he is better I don't suppose it matters.'

It did, however, matter very much, for it showed that the patient's own thoughts or imagination were quite capable of causing a serious condition which had been labelled 'asthma' and which had resisted all orthodox treatment. It showed equally clearly that the patient's own imagination was quite capable of bringing about a cure once it could be directed along the right lines.

I quote this case at length, too, because it points so many morals! This typical case of the chronic asthma was clearly started by the patient's own imagination, and as soon as he realised it he cured himself.

There was no 'sleep talk' or hypnotic-eye nonsense, just hypnosis, although unrecognised as such by the patient. The old man's very belligerence showed him to be particularly suggestible.

If he only knew it, Colonel —— would have been the almost perfect subject for the old-fashioned deep-trance hypnotism! Imagining the hypnotist had extraordinary powers, and concentrating his mind to be on guard against falling under his 'spell,' the gallant colonel had really absorbed the explanations so well that they acted with the force of a hypnotic suggestion! Such a quick result is, however, quite exceptional. This method of treatment is not advised, but it was the only one possible under the unusual circumstances.

Chapter Forty

THE CASE OF THE DITHERER

IF WE WERE able to give every driver and every pedestrian a brief course of hypnosis there would be very few road accidents. This bold claim is based on experience, for recorded in the archives of the British Society of Medical Hypnotists are numerous cases in which accident-prone people have been reformed.

As we saw in Chapter 23 even a careless garage mechanic has been turned into a careful and conscientious worker so that never again is he likely to leave a nut untightened or brakes badly adjusted.

Here are two typical examples of what has been done.

Mrs. ——, a middle-aged married woman, was a ditherer *de luxe*. She was sent by her doctor for hypnotic treatment, as it seemed nothing could be done to cure her obsession that she must do everything over and over again 'just to make sure.'

She would lock her front door, for instance, and return time and again to test it.

Often while crossing the road she would stop suddenly and dash back—while brakes squealed and drivers cursed.

Her mind was concentrated by hypnosis after the relaxation routine, and she suddenly remembered how it had all started.

As a child approaching adolescence, she had passed through a stage of being clumsy and forgetful.

'Do be careful!' and 'Don't forget!' were the words constantly dinned into her ears by her mother. They were even shouted at her as she went to school.

One morning, half-way across the road, the maternal shout reminded her that she had indeed forgotten something. The child wheeled round—and recovered consciousness in an ambulance.

'That's what comes of forgetting!' was the mother's remark

at their highly emotional reunion. She had been afraid of forgetting ever since.

After that piece of self-revelation the treatment began to take effect; she is not only free of her stupid obsession—she is a model pedestrian!

Here, surely, is something for the Minister of Transport to investigate. Since every new driver is subjected to an individual driving test for an hour or so, there can be no practical opposition to the idea of adding a little hypnosis with suggestions directed towards kindness, care and courtesy!

Chapter Forty-one

THE CASE OF THE LAWYER

For a lawyer to wink at a magistrate during a trial is more than a breach of good manners—it is contempt of court!

Mr. ——, a brilliant young solicitor, not only did it often, he just could not stop.

He would wink slowly and deliberately, when in conference with clients, usually at the most serious stage of the discussion.

This was bad for professional work, and his hopes of a junior partnership faded.

His doctor tried drugs, eye exercises, massage and tonics without effect, and finally recommended hypnotherapy as a last hope.

At the end of the second session of hypnosis the following suggestion was given.

'Now you have learned to relax your mind and body you will remember during the next few days what started this winking.'

The next week, Mr. —— related the following incident of his schooldays.

A teacher who caught young —— winking at a companion hauled the lad out in front of the class and 'raved and ranted.' Young ——, he shouted, looked 'like a silly ass, blinking like an owl.' Only sly, unpleasant characters couldn't keep their eyes from blinking and winking—and so on, until the lad was in a high state of emotional embarrassment.

As a punishment, —— was told to stand in front of the class and stare without blinking for five minutes by the classroom clock.

Of course, he could not do it, and he was ridiculed for his failure. Shame and resentment overwhelmed every other thought.

Years later, as a promising young solicitor, he got a fact

wrong while defending a client in the police court, and the magistrate was heavily sarcastic.

Ashamed and resentful, Mr. —— started to wink! And the more worried he became, the more his eyelids fluttered. So another vicious circle was established and an unfortunate habit-spasm born.

The patient was astonished to learn that a teacher's bad temper could have such serious effects many years later, but he readily agreed that it was silly to let it go on. And Mr. —— has not winked—involuntarily—since.

One is forced to the conclusion that if only teachers (and perhaps magistrates!) would undergo hypnosis during their training, bad tempers directed at the young could be abolished and much unhappiness in later life avoided.

Chapter Forty-two

THE CASE OF THE NON-SMOKER

PEOPLE ARE KILLED by fear as well as by disease germs. At least 60 per cent of the medical certificates issued by general practitioners should have the word 'fear' written on the dotted line following the words 'is suffering from . . .'

Mostly, the fear is groundless and the patient has long since forgotten what it was. Yet it can bring illness and even death.

Several times in recent years a possible connection between cigarette smoking and lung cancer has been headlined in newspapers; but what general practitioner could be expected to link up one of these scares with the illness of Mr. ——, a non-smoker?

Mr. ——'s symptoms were not unusual; he was run down, could not sleep, had fits of panic, headaches and impaired memory. Nothing definite, you see, just a general sort of illness that got steadily worse and worse. His work suffered, he feared unemployment, and he was rapidly becoming a mental and physical wreck.

The trouble was detected after treatment by hypnosis, when the patient was shown how to relax and to concentrate his mind.

He remembered then, quite clearly, how it had all started.

A non-smoker himself, his wife was 'a perfect chimney'; and one of the annual cancer scares happened at a time when Mrs. —— developed mysterious pains in the chest.

Mr. —— woke up one night bathed in perspiration. His wife, he was suddenly convinced, must have lung cancer—through smoking!

He dared not tell her of his fear; he kept it bottled up. The worry and anxiety created a state of nervous tension; he had developed insomnia, short temper and bad memory, and the more he worried about his condition the worse his symptoms became. In fact, he was so concerned with his own troubles that he appeared to take little notice of the discovery that his wife's chest pains were simply caused by indigestion.

By remembering these things and getting the whole story in its right perspective, Mr. —— helped to overthrow his neurosis. The relaxation he learned under hypnosis soon dispelled the tension, the vicious circle was broken and his recovery was rapid.

When Mrs. —— learned the truth, she underwent a course of treatment herself and gave up smoking!

Chapter Forty-three

THE CASE OF CINDERELLA

IN A WOMAN, a blush can be an enchantment—or an embarrassment. A boyish figure can be elegant—or just undeveloped.

It all depends on the way you look at it.

Miss —— looked upon herself without enthusiasm.
She was thin and flat-chested, and her lank, untidy hair
framed a pale, perplexed face. She was quietly, perhaps
dowdily, dressed—a little London suburban mouse very much
afraid of life.

Migraine, she said, was her trouble—searing, throbbing
headaches that made life a misery in the dismal, dusty office
where she worked and in the conventional suburban villa
where she slept.

There was no organic cause, of course. Over the years, her
doctor had probed the problem unremittingly, and drugs had
given only temporary relief.

Eventually she was sent for medical hypnosis.

We do not always need to dig far back into the past to
discover the cause of nervous ills. Sometimes the present is
all too obviously responsible. It certainly was so in the case of
Miss ——.

She was burdened with a gay and colourful sister, a glamour
puss who had shone at school as a peaches-and-cream child
basking blissfully in the limelight of social precocity.

'If only you were like your sister,' her mother would persist
in despondent tones. 'You've got no "go" in you.'

While sister blossomed through the years of adolescence,
Miss —— shrank farther back into herself.

Sister had boy friends; Miss —— felt like crawling under the
table when a masculine step was heard upon the path.

Sister went dancing; Miss —— washed up. Sister's job was a
pleasure, Miss ——'s was a purgatory.

'If only you were like your sister' became the familiar phrase whenever Cinderella put in an appearance.

Anyone taking the trouble to look closely at Miss —— would have noted that she was by no means bad-looking under the mask of weary resignation. The bone structure of her face was good.

But then no one could look closely at Miss —— without her face blushing alarmingly, and you felt that even her mind was trembling.

The Chinese have a saying: 'A picture is better than a thousand words.'

So, under waking hypnosis, Miss —— was shown a mental picture—a glowing reel of imaginary CinemaScope in glorious, pulsating Technicolor.

'This isn't how you could be—it's how you *will* be,' she was told.

The idea was developed during treatment. Miss —— saw herself lovable and affectionate, a welcome companion and the cherished friend of many. People wanted to be with her because she was gay and generous, wise and good.

Broad hints were dropped. Why wear such frumpish clothes? They didn't go with her real—and hitherto hidden—personality. A shopping expedition was prescribed.

And that hair! A good hairdresser could make it soft and charming. She owed it to her friends to make the best of herself.

Buy a new hat, she was told—lots of new hats. Have a facial —lots of facials.

From the very beginning of her treatment Miss —— began to blossom.

The very first hair-do and touch of cosmetic colour in her cheeks was a promising start.

But the effect on Miss ——'s mind was the most rewarding. She threw off her cloak of wistful woe and sang happily round the house.

She still washed up—but visitors made a beeline for the kitchen.

So the Cinderella story came true. A regular, if unconventional, form of treatment had again succeeded.

Miss —— is engaged to be married now, and she finds life full of promise.

The migraines? She has forgotten all about them. They ceased to be important from the day she saw that colourful mind-movie starring the glamorous Miss ——.

Those headaches were not physical, you see. They were just Nature's way of rebelling against the family catch-phrase.

Chapter Forty-four

THE CASE OF THE POLICEMAN

INSOMNIA IS ONE of the commonest symptoms of nervous tension, and I have yet to hear of anyone who has cured himself by counting sheep.

But what of people who cannot keep awake?

P.C. —— came into this category, and it had haunted him since adolescence. At school he would drop off to sleep in class, to the amusement of his classmates and the annoyance of his teachers. They called him 'Dreamy Daniel.'

The habit persisted through the many jobs he tried to keep. He joined the police force in the hope that the active, open-air life would keep him conscious.

But it was not long before a sergeant found him propped up against a lamp-post—fast asleep. He got out of immediate trouble by claiming illness, and after a brief holiday on sick leave he developed considerable cunning in arranging to have his 'forty winks' on duty by retiring into those strategic places (public conveniences) where those in authority were unlikely to follow.

Fortunately, P.C. —— realised in time that there was a limit to his luck, when incidents happened too often when he was not around and patrolling sergeants began to doubt his explanations.

His doctor sent him to the hypnotherapist.

The son of a tea planter in Ceylon, —— had enjoyed a happy and uneventful childhood. As far as he could remember, the urge to fall asleep at odd and inconvenient moments had started when he was sent home to England at the age of ten.

Physically, he appeared to be in excellent trim; his mind was active and his intelligence above average. There was no obvious explanation for his trouble.

The explanation came, in the usual way, when under

hypnosis he was told that he would remember some event, or experience, in his early life that would account for his condition.

As a child, he recalled, he was exceptionally active, and on his father's tea plantation there were animals and toys and every 'incentive to play around.

But his parents, as is usual in the tropics, were addicted to the afternoon siesta, and little ——'s playful habits were not appreciated at such times.

If he did not sleep in the afternoon, he would get sick and die, he was told—unwisely, perhaps, but understandably.

Nobody explained why it was desirable to take a siesta in the tropics; it was just a parental instruction. But after a period of rebellion he accepted the situation and conformed to custom.

His young mind must have been puzzled and perplexed when he found that siestas were not the thing in England. He did not want to 'get sick and die,' so, whether it was the thing or not, the occasional 'forty winks' became an essential protection.

And so it proved that P.C. ——'s unofficial naps were the blind obedience to a parental injunction, and once this was explained to him he had no further trouble.

He drives a car these days, and never has the slightest tendency to fall asleep at the wheel.

One wonders how many road accidents caused by drivers falling asleep could be traced to overstatement of the case for afternoon naps for the very young!

Chapter Forty-five

THE CASE OF THE PARSON

THROAT SPECIALISTS FAILED to discover any physical cause for the Rev. ——'s loss of voice. A married man of over fifty, he had enjoyed a long and successful ministry in a suburban church until his voice started to go.

It was a very worried parson who finally sought relief in hypnotherapy 'as a last resort.'

He suspected that the trouble was psychological, he explained, because it had started about the time he experienced an irresistible urge to use a certain colourful and unpriestly expletive in the pulpit.

Normally, his voice was strong and resonant, his sermons forceful. Imagine, therefore, his distress when, as the theme of his discourse developed and approached the proper dramatic climax, the word would haunt his lips until it spilled right out in place of the adjective he intended.

The first time it happened, he stopped in mid-syllable and turned it into blu-u-ntly. Another time he succeeded in describing a Biblical murderer as bl-l-issful. Any sin was liable to become bl-l-essed!

He began to fear the Sunday services; his voice lost its confident resonance, became hoarse and hesitant. When he first reported for treatment, he spoke only in a whisper.

Rightly enough, he associated his loss of voice with his urge to swear. But that was the limit of his psychological understanding.

It was explained to him that the impulse to use the forbidden word was symptomatic of nervous tension. He may have forgotten what caused it, for people often repress unpleasant experiences with mental cotton wool as an oyster covers up the irritating grain of sand. But under hypnosis he would remember.

A PERSONAL WORD FROM MELVIN POWERS
PUBLISHER, WILSHIRE BOOK COMPANY

Dear Friend:

My goal is to publish interesting, informative, and inspirational books. You can help me accomplish this by answering the following questions, either by phone or by mail. Or, if convenient for you, I would welcome the opportunity to visit with you in my office and hear your comments in person.

Did you enjoy reading this book? Why?

Would you enjoy reading another similar book?

What idea in the book impressed you the most?

If applicable to your situation, have you incorporated this idea in your daily life?

Is there a chapter that could serve as a theme for an entire book? Please explain.

If you have an idea for a book, I would welcome discussing it with you. If you already have one in progress, write or call me concerning possible publication. I can be reached at (213) 875-1711 or (213) 983-1105.

Sincerely yours,

MELVIN POWERS

12015 Sherman Road
North Hollywood, California 91605

MELVIN POWERS SELF-IMPROVEMENT LIBRARY

ASTROLOGY

____ ASTROLOGY: HOW TO CHART YOUR HOROSCOPE *Max Heindel*	3.00
____ ASTROLOGY: YOUR PERSONAL SUN-SIGN GUIDE *Beatrice Ryder*	3.00
____ ASTROLOGY FOR EVERYDAY LIVING *Janet Harris*	2.00
____ ASTROLOGY MADE EASY *Astarte*	3.00
____ ASTROLOGY MADE PRACTICAL *Alexandra Kayhle*	3.00
____ ASTROLOGY, ROMANCE, YOU AND THE STARS *Anthony Norvell*	4.00
____ MY WORLD OF ASTROLOGY *Sydney Omarr*	5.00
____ THOUGHT DIAL *Sidney Omarr*	4.00
____ WHAT THE STARS REVEAL ABOUT THE MEN IN YOUR LIFE *Thelma White*	3.00

BRIDGE

____ BRIDGE BIDDING MADE EASY *Edwin B. Kantar*	7.00
____ BRIDGE CONVENTIONS *Edwin B. Kantar*	7.00
____ BRIDGE HUMOR *Edwin B. Kantar*	5.00
____ COMPETITIVE BIDDING IN MODERN BRIDGE *Edgar Kaplan*	4.00
____ DEFENSIVE BRIDGE PLAY COMPLETE *Edwin B. Kantar*	10.00
____ GAMESMAN BRIDGE—Play Better with Kantar *Edwin B. Kantar*	5.00
____ HOW TO IMPROVE YOUR BRIDGE *Alfred Sheinwold*	5.00
____ IMPROVING YOUR BIDDING SKILLS *Edwin B. Kantar*	4.00
____ INTRODUCTION TO DEFENDER'S PLAY *Edwin B. Kantar*	3.00
____ KANTAR FOR THE DEFENSE *Edwin B. Kantar*	5.00
____ SHORT CUT TO WINNING BRIDGE *Alfred Sheinwold*	3.00
____ TEST YOUR BRIDGE PLAY *Edwin B. Kantar*	5.00
____ VOLUME 2—TEST YOUR BRIDGE PLAY *Edwin B. Kantar*	5.00
____ WINNING DECLARER PLAY *Dorothy Hayden Truscott*	4.00

BUSINESS, STUDY & REFERENCE

____ CONVERSATION MADE EASY *Elliot Russell*	3.00
____ EXAM SECRET *Dennis B. Jackson*	3.00
____ FIX-IT BOOK *Arthur Symons*	2.00
____ HOW TO DEVELOP A BETTER SPEAKING VOICE *M. Hellier*	3.00
____ HOW TO MAKE A FORTUNE IN REAL ESTATE *Albert Winnikoff*	4.00
____ INCREASE YOUR LEARNING POWER *Geoffrey A. Dudley*	3.00
____ MAGIC OF NUMBERS *Robert Tocquet*	2.00
____ PRACTICAL GUIDE TO BETTER CONCENTRATION *Melvin Powers*	3.00
____ PRACTICAL GUIDE TO PUBLIC SPEAKING *Maurice Forley*	3.00
____ 7 DAYS TO FASTER READING *William S. Schaill*	3.00
____ SONGWRITERS' RHYMING DICTIONARY *Jane Shaw Whitfield*	5.00
____ SPELLING MADE EASY *Lester D. Basch & Dr. Milton Finkelstein*	3.00
____ STUDENT'S GUIDE TO BETTER GRADES *J. A. Rickard*	3.00
____ TEST YOURSELF—Find Your Hidden Talent *Jack Shafer*	3.00
____ YOUR WILL & WHAT TO DO ABOUT IT *Attorney Samuel G. Kling*	3.00

CALLIGRAPHY

____ ADVANCED CALLIGRAPHY *Katherine Jeffares*	7.00
____ CALLIGRAPHER'S REFERENCE BOOK *Anne Leptich & Jacque Evans*	7.00
____ CALLIGRAPHY—The Art of Beautiful Writing *Katherine Jeffares*	7.00
____ CALLIGRAPHY FOR FUN & PROFIT *Anne Leptich & Jacque Evans*	7.00
____ CALLIGRAPHY MADE EASY *Tina Serafini*	7.00

CHESS & CHECKERS

____ BEGINNER'S GUIDE TO WINNING CHESS *Fred Reinfeld*	3.00
____ CHECKERS MADE EASY *Tom Wiswell*	2.00
____ CHESS IN TEN EASY LESSONS *Larry Evans*	3.00
____ CHESS MADE EASY *Milton L. Hanauer*	3.00
____ CHESS PROBLEMS FOR BEGINNERS *edited by Fred Reinfeld*	2.00
____ CHESS SECRETS REVEALED *Fred Reinfeld*	2.00
____ CHESS STRATEGY—An Expert's Guide *Fred Reinfeld*	2.00
____ CHESS TACTICS FOR BEGINNERS *edited by Fred Reinfeld*	3.00
____ CHESS THEORY & PRACTICE *Morry & Mitchell*	2.00
____ HOW TO WIN AT CHECKERS *Fred Reinfeld*	3.00
____ 1001 BRILLIANT WAYS TO CHECKMATE *Fred Reinfeld*	4.00
____ 1001 WINNING CHESS SACRIFICES & COMBINATIONS *Fred Reinfeld*	4.00
____ SOVIET CHESS *Edited by R. G. Wade*	3.00

COOKERY & HERBS

____ CULPEPER'S HERBAL REMEDIES *Dr. Nicholas Culpeper*	3.00
____ FAST GOURMET COOKBOOK *Poppy Cannon*	2.50
____ GINSENG The Myth & The Truth *Joseph P. Hou*	3.00
____ HEALING POWER OF HERBS *May Bethel*	4.00
____ HEALING POWER OF NATURAL FOODS *May Bethel*	3.00
____ HERB HANDBOOK *Dawn MacLeod*	3.00
____ HERBS FOR COOKING AND HEALING *Dr. Donald Law*	2.00
____ HERBS FOR HEALTH—How to Grow & Use Them *Louise Evans Doole*	3.00
____ HOME GARDEN COOKBOOK—Delicious Natural Food Recipes *Ken Kraft*	3.00
____ MEDICAL HERBALIST *edited by Dr. J. R. Yemm*	3.00
____ NATURAL FOOD COOKBOOK *Dr. Harry C. Bond*	3.00
____ NATURE'S MEDICINES *Richard Lucas*	3.00
____ VEGETABLE GARDENING FOR BEGINNERS *Hugh Wiberg*	2.00
____ VEGETABLES FOR TODAY'S GARDENS *R. Milton Carleton*	2.00
____ VEGETARIAN COOKERY *Janet Walker*	4.00
____ VEGETARIAN COOKING MADE EASY & DELECTABLE *Veronica Vezza*	3.00
____ VEGETARIAN DELIGHTS—A Happy Cookbook for Health *K. R. Mehta*	2.00
____ VEGETARIAN GOURMET COOKBOOK *Joyce McKinnel*	3.00

GAMBLING & POKER

____ ADVANCED POKER STRATEGY & WINNING PLAY *A. D. Livingston*	5.00
____ HOW NOT TO LOSE AT POKER *Jeffrey Lloyd Castle*	3.00
____ HOW TO WIN AT DICE GAMES *Skip Frey*	3.00
____ HOW TO WIN AT POKER *Terence Reese & Anthony T. Watkins*	3.00
____ SECRETS OF WINNING POKER *George S. Coffin*	3.00
____ WINNING AT CRAPS *Dr. Lloyd T. Commins*	3.00
____ WINNING AT GIN *Chester Wander & Cy Rice*	3.00
____ WINNING AT POKER—An Expert's Guide *John Archer*	3.00
____ WINNING AT 21—An Expert's Guide *John Archer*	5.00
____ WINNING POKER SYSTEMS *Norman Zadeh*	3.00

HEALTH

____ BEE POLLEN *Lynda Lyngheim & Jack Scagnetti*	3.00
____ DR. LINDNER'S SPECIAL WEIGHT CONTROL METHOD *P. G. Lindner, M.D.*	1.50
____ HELP YOURSELF TO BETTER SIGHT *Margaret Darst Corbett*	3.00
____ HOW TO IMPROVE YOUR VISION *Dr. Robert A. Kraskin*	3.00
____ HOW YOU CAN STOP SMOKING PERMANENTLY *Ernest Caldwell*	3.00
____ MIND OVER PLATTER *Peter G. Lindner, M.D.*	3.00
____ NATURE'S WAY TO NUTRITION & VIBRANT HEALTH *Robert J. Scrutton*	3.00
____ NEW CARBOHYDRATE DIET COUNTER *Patti Lopez-Pereira*	1.50
____ QUICK & EASY EXERCISES FOR FACIAL BEAUTY *Judy Smith-deal*	2.00
____ QUICK & EASY EXERCISES FOR FIGURE BEAUTY *Judy Smith-deal*	2.00
____ REFLEXOLOGY *Dr. Maybelle Segal*	3.00
____ REFLEXOLOGY FOR GOOD HEALTH *Anna Kaye & Don C. Matchan*	3.00
____ YOU CAN LEARN TO RELAX *Dr. Samuel Gutwirth*	3.00
____ YOUR ALLERGY—What To Do About It *Allan Knight, M.D.*	3.00

HOBBIES

____ BEACHCOMBING FOR BEGINNERS *Norman Hickin*	2.00
____ BLACKSTONE'S MODERN CARD TRICKS *Harry Blackstone*	3.00
____ BLACKSTONE'S SECRETS OF MAGIC *Harry Blackstone*	3.00
____ COIN COLLECTING FOR BEGINNERS *Burton Hobson & Fred Reinfeld*	3.00
____ ENTERTAINING WITH ESP *Tony 'Doc' Shiels*	2.00
____ 400 FASCINATING MAGIC TRICKS YOU CAN DO *Howard Thurston*	4.00
____ HOW I TURN JUNK INTO FUN AND PROFIT *Sari*	3.00
____ HOW TO WRITE A HIT SONG & SELL IT *Tommy Boyce*	7.00
____ JUGGLING MADE EASY *Rudolf Dittrich*	2.00
____ MAGIC FOR ALL AGES *Walter Gibson*	4.00
____ MAGIC MADE EASY *Byron Wels*	2.00
____ STAMP COLLECTING FOR BEGINNERS *Burton Hobson*	3.00

HORSE PLAYERS' WINNING GUIDES

____ BETTING HORSES TO WIN *Les Conklin*	3.00
____ ELIMINATE THE LOSERS *Bob McKnight*	3.00
____ HOW TO PICK WINNING HORSES *Bob McKnight*	3.00

____ HOW TO WIN AT THE RACES *Sam (The Genius) Lewin*		5.00
____ HOW YOU CAN BEAT THE RACES *Jack Kavanagh*		3.00
____ MAKING MONEY AT THE RACES *David Barr*		3.00
____ PAYDAY AT THE RACES *Les Conklin*		3.00
____ SMART HANDICAPPING MADE EASY *William Bauman*		3.00
____ SUCCESS AT THE HARNESS RACES *Barry Meadow*		3.00
____ WINNING AT THE HARNESS RACES—An Expert's Guide *Nick Cammarano*		3.00

HUMOR

____ HOW TO BE A COMEDIAN FOR FUN & PROFIT *King & Laufer*		2.00
____ HOW TO FLATTEN YOUR TUSH *Coach Marge Reardon*		2.00
____ HOW TO MAKE LOVE TO YOURSELF *Ron Stevens & Joy Grdnic*		3.00
____ JOKE TELLER'S HANDBOOK *Bob Orben*		3.00
____ JOKES FOR ALL OCCASIONS *Al Schock*		3.00
____ 2000 NEW LAUGHS FOR SPEAKERS *Bob Orben*		4.00
____ 2,500 JOKES TO START 'EM LAUGHING *Bob Orben*		3.00

HYPNOTISM

____ ADVANCED TECHNIQUES OF HYPNOSIS *Melvin Powers*		2.00
____ BRAINWASHING AND THE CULTS *Paul A. Verdier, Ph.D.*		3.00
____ CHILDBIRTH WITH HYPNOSIS *William S. Kroger, M.D.*		5.00
____ HOW TO SOLVE Your Sex Problems with Self-Hypnosis *Frank S. Caprio, M.D.*		5.00
____ HOW TO STOP SMOKING THRU SELF-HYPNOSIS *Leslie M. LeCron*		3.00
____ HOW TO USE AUTO-SUGGESTION EFFECTIVELY *John Duckworth*		3.00
____ HOW YOU CAN BOWL BETTER USING SELF-HYPNOSIS *Jack Heise*		3.00
____ HOW YOU CAN PLAY BETTER GOLF USING SELF-HYPNOSIS *Jack Heise*		3.00
____ HYPNOSIS AND SELF-HYPNOSIS *Bernard Hollander, M.D.*		3.00
____ HYPNOTISM *(Originally published in 1893) Carl Sextus*		5.00
____ HYPNOTISM & PSYCHIC PHENOMENA *Simeon Edmunds*		4.00
____ HYPNOTISM MADE EASY *Dr. Ralph Winn*		3.00
____ HYPNOTISM MADE PRACTICAL *Louis Orton*		3.00
____ HYPNOTISM REVEALED *Melvin Powers*		2.00
____ HYPNOTISM TODAY *Leslie LeCron and Jean Bordeaux, Ph.D.*		5.00
____ MODERN HYPNOSIS *Lesley Kuhn & Salvatore Russo, Ph.D.*		5.00
____ NEW CONCEPTS OF HYPNOSIS *Bernard C. Gindes, M.D.*		5.00
____ NEW SELF-HYPNOSIS *Paul Adams*		4.00
____ POST-HYPNOTIC INSTRUCTIONS—Suggestions for Therapy *Arnold Furst*		3.00
____ PRACTICAL GUIDE TO SELF-HYPNOSIS *Melvin Powers*		3.00
____ PRACTICAL HYPNOTISM *Philip Magonet, M.D.*		3.00
____ SECRETS OF HYPNOTISM *S. J. Van Pelt, M.D.*		5.00
____ SELF-HYPNOSIS A Conditioned-Response Technique *Laurence Sparks*		5.00
____ SELF-HYPNOSIS Its Theory, Technique & Application *Melvin Powers*		3.00
____ THERAPY THROUGH HYPNOSIS *edited by Raphael H. Rhodes*		4.00

JUDAICA

____ HOW TO LIVE A RICHER & FULLER LIFE *Rabbi Edgar F. Magnin*		2.00
____ MODERN ISRAEL *Lily Edelman*		2.00
____ SERVICE OF THE HEART *Evelyn Garfiel, Ph.D.*		4.00
____ STORY OF ISRAEL IN COINS *Jean & Maurice Gould*		2.00
____ STORY OF ISRAEL IN STAMPS *Maxim & Gabriel Shamir*		1.00
____ TONGUE OF THE PROPHETS *Robert St. John*		5.00

JUST FOR WOMEN

____ COSMOPOLITAN'S GUIDE TO MARVELOUS MEN Fwd. by *Helen Gurley Brown*		3.00
____ COSMOPOLITAN'S HANG-UP HANDBOOK Foreword by *Helen Gurley Brown*		4.00
____ COSMOPOLITAN'S LOVE BOOK—A Guide to Ecstasy in Bed		4.00
____ COSMOPOLITAN'S NEW ETIQUETTE GUIDE Fwd. by *Helen Gurley Brown*		4.00
____ I AM A COMPLEAT WOMAN *Doris Hagopian & Karen O'Connor Sweeney*		3.00
____ JUST FOR WOMEN—A Guide to the Female Body *Richard E. Sand, M.D.*		5.00
____ NEW APPROACHES TO SEX IN MARRIAGE *John E. Eichenlaub, M.D.*		3.00
____ SEXUALLY ADEQUATE FEMALE *Frank S. Caprio, M.D.*		3.00
____ YOUR FIRST YEAR OF MARRIAGE *Dr. Tom McGinnis*		3.00

MARRIAGE, SEX & PARENTHOOD

____ ABILITY TO LOVE *Dr. Allan Fromme*		5.00
____ ENCYCLOPEDIA OF MODERN SEX & LOVE TECHNIQUES *Macandrew*		5.00
____ GUIDE TO SUCCESSFUL MARRIAGE *Drs. Albert Ellis & Robert Harper*		5.00

____ MAGIC OF THINKING BIG *Dr. David J. Schwartz*	3.00
____ MAGIC POWER OF YOUR MIND *Walter M. Germain*	5.00
____ MENTAL POWER THROUGH SLEEP SUGGESTION *Melvin Powers*	3.00
____ NEW GUIDE TO RATIONAL LIVING *Albert Ellis, Ph.D. & R. Harper, Ph.D.*	3.00
____ OUR TROUBLED SELVES *Dr. Allan Fromme*	3.00
____ PSYCHO-CYBERNETICS *Maxwell Maltz, M.D.*	3.00
____ SCIENCE OF MIND IN DAILY LIVING *Dr. Donald Curtis*	5.00
____ SECRET OF SECRETS *U. S. Andersen*	5.00
____ SECRET POWER OF THE PYRAMIDS *U. S. Andersen*	5.00
____ STUTTERING AND WHAT YOU CAN DO ABOUT IT *W. Johnson, Ph.D.*	2.50
____ SUCCESS-CYBERNETICS *U. S. Andersen*	5.00
____ 10 DAYS TO A GREAT NEW LIFE *William E. Edwards*	3.00
____ THINK AND GROW RICH *Napoleon Hill*	3.00
____ THINK YOUR WAY TO SUCCESS *Dr. Lew Losoncy*	5.00
____ THREE MAGIC WORDS *U. S. Andersen*	5.00
____ TREASURY OF COMFORT *edited by Rabbi Sidney Greenberg*	5.00
____ TREASURY OF THE ART OF LIVING *Sidney S. Greenberg*	5.00
____ YOU ARE NOT THE TARGET *Laura Huxley*	4.00
____ YOUR SUBCONSCIOUS POWER *Charles M. Simmons*	5.00
____ YOUR THOUGHTS CAN CHANGE YOUR LIFE *Dr. Donald Curtis*	5.00

SPORTS

____ BICYCLING FOR FUN AND GOOD HEALTH *Kenneth E. Luther*	2.00
____ BILLIARDS—Pocket • Carom • Three Cushion *Clive Cottingham, Jr.*	3.00
____ CAMPING-OUT 101 Ideas & Activities *Bruno Knobel*	2.00
____ COMPLETE GUIDE TO FISHING *Vlad Evanoff*	2.00
____ HOW TO IMPROVE YOUR RACQUETBALL *Lubarsky Kaufman & Scagnetti*	3.00
____ HOW TO WIN AT POCKET BILLIARDS *Edward D. Knuchell*	4.00
____ JOY OF WALKING *Jack Scagnetti*	3.00
____ LEARNING & TEACHING SOCCER SKILLS *Eric Worthington*	3.00
____ MOTORCYCLING FOR BEGINNERS *I. G. Edmonds*	3.00
____ RACQUETBALL FOR WOMEN *Toni Hudson, Jack Scagnetti & Vince Rondone*	3.00
____ RACQUETBALL MADE EASY *Steve Lubarsky, Rod Delson & Jack Scagnetti*	3.00
____ SECRET OF BOWLING STRIKES *Dawson Taylor*	3.00
____ SECRET OF PERFECT PUTTING *Horton Smith & Dawson Taylor*	3.00
____ SOCCER—The Game & How to Play It *Gary Rosenthal*	3.00
____ STARTING SOCCER *Edward F. Dolan, Jr.*	3.00
____ TABLE TENNIS MADE EASY *Johnny Leach*	2.00

TENNIS LOVERS' LIBRARY

____ BEGINNER'S BUIDE TO WINNING TENNIS *Helen Hull Jacobs*	2.00
____ HOW TO BEAT BETTER TENNIS PLAYERS *Loring Fiske*	4.00
____ HOW TO IMPROVE YOUR TENNIS—Style, Strategy & Analysis *C. Wilson*	2.00
____ INSIDE TENNIS—Techniques of Winning *Jim Leighton*	3.00
____ PLAY TENNIS WITH ROSEWALL *Ken Rosewall*	2.00
____ PSYCH YOURSELF TO BETTER TENNIS *Dr. Walter A. Luszki*	2.00
____ SUCCESSFUL TENNIS *Neale Fraser*	2.00
____ TENNIS FOR BEGINNERS, *Dr. H. A. Murray*	2.00
____ TENNIS MADE EASY *Joel Brecheen*	3.00
____ WEEKEND TENNIS—How to Have Fun & Win at the Same Time *Bill Talbert*	3.00
____ WINNING WITH PERCENTAGE TENNIS—Smart Strategy *Jack Lowe*	2.00

WILSHIRE PET LIBRARY

____ DOG OBEDIENCE TRAINING *Gust Kessopulos*	4.00
____ DOG TRAINING MADE EASY & FUN *John W. Kellogg*	4.00
____ HOW TO BRING UP YOUR PET DOG *Kurt Unkelbach*	2.00
____ HOW TO RAISE & TRAIN YOUR PUPPY *Jeff Griffen*	3.00
____ PIGEONS: HOW TO RAISE & TRAIN THEM *William H. Allen, Jr.*	2.00

The books listed above can be obtained from your book dealer or directly from Melvin Powers. When ordering, please remit 50¢ per book postage & handling. Send for our free illustrated catalog of self-improvement books.

Melvin Powers

12015 Sherman Road, No. Hollywood, California 91605

WILSHIRE HORSE LOVERS' LIBRARY

_____ AMATEUR HORSE BREEDER *A. C. Leighton Hardman*	4.00
_____ AMERICAN QUARTER HORSE IN PICTURES *Margaret Cabell Self*	3.00
_____ APPALOOSA HORSE *Donna & Bill Richardson*	5.00
_____ ARABIAN HORSE *Reginald S. Summerhays*	3.00
_____ ART OF WESTERN RIDING *Suzanne Norton Jones*	3.00
_____ AT THE HORSE SHOW *Margaret Cabell Self*	3.00
_____ BACK-YARD HORSE *Peggy Jett Pittinger*	4.00
_____ BASIC DRESSAGE *Jean Froissard*	2.00
_____ BEGINNER'S GUIDE TO HORSEBACK RIDING *Sheila Wall*	2.00
_____ BEGINNER'S GUIDE TO THE WESTERN HORSE *Natlee Kenoyer*	2.00
_____ BITS—THEIR HISTORY, USE AND MISUSE *Louis Taylor*	5.00
_____ BREAKING & TRAINING THE DRIVING HORSE *Doris Ganton*	3.00
_____ BREAKING YOUR HORSE'S BAD HABITS *W. Dayton Sumner*	4.00
_____ COMPLETE TRAINING OF HORSE AND RIDER *Colonel Alois Podhajsky*	5.00
_____ DISORDERS OF THE HORSE & WHAT TO DO ABOUT THEM *E. Hanauer*	3.00
_____ DOG TRAINING MADE EASY & FUN *John W. Kellogg*	4.00
_____ DRESSAGE—A Study of the Finer Points in Riding *Henry Wynmalen*	5.00
_____ DRIVE ON *Doris Ganton*	7.00
_____ DRIVING HORSES *Sallie Walrond*	3.00
_____ ENDURANCE RIDING *Ann Hyland*	2.00
_____ EQUITATION *Jean Froissard*	5.00
_____ FIRST AID FOR HORSES *Dr. Charles H. Denning, Jr.*	3.00
_____ FUN OF RAISING A COLT *Rubye & Frank Griffith*	3.00
_____ FUN ON HORSEBACK *Margaret Caball Self*	4.00
_____ GYMKHANA GAMES *Natlee Kenoyer*	2.00
_____ HORSE DISEASES—Causes, Symptoms & Treatment *Dr. H. G. Belschner*	5.00
_____ HORSE OWNER'S CONCISE GUIDE *Elsie V. Hanauer*	2.00
_____ HORSE SELECTION & CARE FOR BEGINNERS *George H. Conn*	5.00
_____ HORSEBACK RIDING FOR BEGINNERS *Louis Taylor*	5.00
_____ HORSEBACK RIDING MADE EASY & FUN *Sue Henderson Coen*	5.00
_____ HORSES—Their Selection, Care & Handling *Margaret Cabell Self*	4.00
_____ HOW TO BUY A BETTER HORSE & SELL THE HORSE YOU OWN	3.00
_____ HOW TO ENJOY YOUR QUARTER HORSE *Willard H. Porter*	3.00
_____ HUNTER IN PICTURES *Margaret Cabell Self*	2.00
_____ ILLUSTRATED BOOK OF THE HORSE *S. Sidney* (8½" × 11")	10.00
_____ ILLUSTRATED HORSE MANAGEMENT—400 Illustrations *Dr. E. Mayhew*	6.00
_____ ILLUSTRATED HORSE TRAINING *Captain M. H. Hayes*	5.00
_____ ILLUSTRATED HORSEBACK RIDING FOR BEGINNERS *Jeanne Mellin*	3.00
_____ JUMPING—Learning & Teaching *Jean Froissard*	4.00
_____ KNOW ALL ABOUT HORSES *Harry Disston*	3.00
_____ LAME HORSE Cause, Symptoms & Treatment *Dr. James R. Rooney*	4.00
_____ LAW & YOUR HORSE *Edward H. Greene*	5.00
_____ LIPIZZANERS & THE SPANISH RIDING SCHOOL *W. Reuter* (4¼" × 6")	2.50
_____ MANUAL OF HORSEMANSHIP *Harold Black*	5.00
_____ MOVIE HORSES—The Fascinating Techniques of Training *Anthony Amaral*	2.00
_____ POLICE HORSES *Judith Campbell*	2.00
_____ PRACTICAL GUIDE TO HORSESHOEING	3.00
_____ PRACTICAL GUIDE TO OWNING YOUR OWN HORSE *Steven D. Price*	3.00
_____ PRACTICAL HORSE PSYCHOLOGY *Moyra Williams*	4.00
_____ PROBLEM HORSES Guide for Curing Serious Behavior Habits *Summerhays*	3.00
_____ REINSMAN OF THE WEST—BRIDLES & BITS *Ed Connell*	5.00
_____ RESCHOOLING THE THOROUGHBRED *Peggy Jett Pittenger*	3.00
_____ RIDE WESTERN *Louis Taylor*	4.00
_____ SCHOOLING YOUR YOUNG HORSE *George Wheatley*	3.00
_____ STABLE MANAGEMENT FOR THE OWNER-GROOM *George Wheatley*	4.00
_____ STALLION MANAGEMENT—A Guide for Stud Owners *A. C. Hardman*	3.00
_____ TEACHING YOUR HORSE TO JUMP *W. J. Froud*	2.00
_____ TRAIL HORSES & TRAIL RIDING *Anne & Perry Westbrook*	2.00
_____ TRAINING YOUR HORSE TO SHOW *Neale Haley*	4.00
_____ TREATING COMMON DISEASES OF YOUR HORSE *Dr. George H. Conn*	3.00
_____ TREATING HORSE AILMENTS *G. W. Serth*	2.00
_____ YOU AND YOUR PONY *Pepper Mainwaring Healey* (8½" × 11")	6.00
_____ YOUR FIRST HORSE *George C. Saunders, M.D.*	3.00
_____ YOUR PONY BOOK *Hermann Wiederhold*	2.00

The books listed above can be obtained from your book dealer or directly from
Melvin Powers. When ordering, please remit 50¢ per book postage & handling.
Send for our free illustrated catalog of self-improvement books.

Melvin Powers
12015 Sherman Road, No. Hollywood, California 91605